Tent Show

NUMBER SIX:
West Texas A&M University Series
Gerald A. Craven, General Editor

DONALD W. WHISENHUNT

TENT SHOW

Arthur Names and His "Famous" Players

Introduction by W. Kenneth Waters, Jr.

Texas A&M University Press
College Station

The paper used in this book meets the minimum requirements
of the American National Standard for Permanence
of Paper for Printed Library Materials, z39.48-1984.
Binding materials have been chosen for durability.
∞

LIBRARY OF CONGRESS CATALOGING-IN-PUBLICATION DATA

Whisenhunt, Donald W.
Tent show : Arthur Names and his "famous" players /
Donald W. Whisenhunt.
p. cm.—(West Texas A&M University series ; no. 6)
Includes bibliographical references and index.
ISBN 0-89096-954-X (cloth)
1. Arthur Names and His Famous Players (Theater group)—
History. 2. Repertory theater—Southwestern states—History—
20th century. 3. Names, Arthur.   I. Title. II. Series.

PN2297.A78 W49 2000
792'.0976'09041—dc21

00-029933

For my brothers,

KENNETH *and* LEWIS WHISENHUNT,

who lived the life and had the experience
for a short time

CONTENTS

THIS MANUSCRIPT IS THE CULMINATION OF MORE THAN TWENTY-five years of research and interest in this subject. As the reader will quickly determine, this story has a strong personal connection. My father was a partner of Arthur Names for a few years, and I have vague and intermittent memories of the tent show. Since both Names and my father died young, they never had a chance to tell their own personal stories of the tent show.

This period of my family's history has always been important to my mother and my brothers. We have talked about Art Names many times through the years. We thought we knew most of the details of the period when my father was involved with the show. We were all surprised when some of the documentary evidence I uncovered contradicted our memories.

After I became a professional historian, I decided to examine the tent show in a scholarly way. I began in 1972 trying to find people who remembered Art Names and to locate surviving members of his family. I was very gratified that many people responded to my pleas for information. I was also able to locate the surviving members of the Names family.

Just as I was getting into the research, I accepted a position in academic administration. The time I had available changed significantly, and I could not work on the project as I had planned. I was able to conduct interviews with Art Names's former wife and their twin sons. The oldest son, Art, Jr., was not interested in the project. I was also able to contact Milburn Stone and conduct an extensive interview with him.

I found that the former Mrs. Names had in her possession two wardrobe trunks full of documents regarding the traveling tent show and her life with Names. I could not convince her to donate this material to an archival repository, but she did give me permission to read and copy the material and to use whatever I found helpful for this manuscript. I spent several days making my own microfilm of the material in the trunks.

Through the years, my research was in a filing cabinet. It seemed to be calling me, but I was never able to get back to it in an extended fashion. I did publish one article in the West Texas Historical Association *Year Book* in 1994, which won the best article award that year. I longed to have the time to work on this project in a more organized way.

That opportunity came when I left academic administration after eighteen years and became a member of the history faculty at Western Washington University. I had one other project that took priority over this one, and I finished it first. Then, finally, it was back to Art Names.

I have explained this in some detail so the reader will be aware of my personal connection to this story and so that the age of the interviews and correspondence from acquaintances of Names is understood. I feel fortunate to have gotten the interviews and the letters from people since many, if not most, of them have passed from the scene since I started this.

Most of the information on the Whisenhunt family comes from oral tradition. The experience with Names was very important and was spoken about often. I did do formal interviews with my two brothers and with my mother before her death in 1991. I was able to ask specific questions, especially about factual materials. Even so, much of the material about my family cannot be documented in the normal way.

In a project of this sort, many people provide assistance, and I have debts that I can never pay. I am especially grateful to Maurine Names Worthington and to Jack and Jean Names for the interviews they granted me and for making the papers of Art Names available. Although he has long since died, I still owe much to Milburn Stone for his memories of the early years of the Art Names Show. My mother and two brothers clearly were important sources, and I owe them for their help. A large number of people corresponded with me in 1973 and are acknowledged in the notes. Without the information they provided, this story would have more gaps that it does. Above all, I want to single out and thank a woman from McCracken, Kansas, whom I have never met. Carolyn Thompson provided me with information that I would never have had otherwise. She assisted me in the 1970s and then again in the 1990s. Despite the interruptions in this project, she continued to help me even when, I am sure, she believed it would never be completed. She did this unselfishly because she loves her hometown and wants this story told. Carolyn, thank you very much.

My immediate family has lived with Art Names for many years. My wife, Betsy, and my two sons, Donald, Jr., and Ben, deserve some credit for the completion of this project: weary of hearing about Names, they pushed me to finish the manuscript. Special thanks must go to my wife, Betsy, as always, since she is the one who has stood by me and encouraged me in all that I have done for almost forty years. Her part in this manuscript is not obvious, but it is there.

Tent Show

Introduction

IN THIS WORK, DONALD W. WHISENHUNT REVEALS MANY OF THE trials and tribulations the small company of players that made up Arthur Names and His "Famous" Players faced as it toured through western Kansas, eastern Colorado, the Oklahoma panhandle, and northwestern Texas. Certainly, such problems had not been unusual for practitioners of the theatrical art prior to the 1920s and 1930s, for the theater had faced both enthusiasm and antagonism from its earliest times on the North American continent.

Theater, with other arts, has had a varied and often tenuous existence in the United States. Unlike European theater, the arts in this country, until fairly recently, have not enjoyed governmental support but have had to be self-sustaining, relying principally on box-office receipts. In many areas of the country, in fact, the arts and theater in particular have faced social rejection and been seen as purveyors of immorality and godlessness. In colonial America, most notably in the New England states, theater was frowned upon as an activity that would contribute to the delinquency of a populace that had far more important matters to consider. It was seen as a European influence directly tied to courts, courtiers, and dilettantes from a society made up of well-defined social classes and was perceived as being anathema to the democratic spirit of a newly formed nation.

John Quincy Adams warned of the dangers of this art form, which he admitted was agreeable but, he said, required an aristocracy where patrons would be available. Therefore, he felt that theater and other activities related to it were not suitable for a democracy. What is more, he condemned the artists when he asked, "Why is it that artists ... renounce their pleasures, neglect their exercise, and destroy their health—for what? Their universal object and idol is ... *reputation.* It is the notoriety, the celebration, which constitutes the charm that is to compensate for the loss of appetite and sleep, and sometimes of riches and honor ... Men of letters must have a good deal of praise."[1]

Benjamin Franklin, far more liberal than Adams, found poetry, music, and the stage to be proper for a refined state of society. However, he did not believe that the society in the United States fit such a definition; and, though one might find the arts enjoyable, such a young nation could hardly afford them.

For George Washington, the art of the drama could be a "chief refiner" of manners, helping a young and roughshod people to "polish the manners and habits of society."[2] However, he observed, a young nation had other, more important priorities.

For these gentlemen and others of this time period, the true arts were utilitarian, "arts" that could make life and living possible in a country still uncivilized and untamed. Franklin observed that "nothing is good or beautiful but in the measure that it is useful."[3] Certainly, therefore, the arts—theater, music, dance, and painting—did not deserve the public or governmental support they enjoyed in Europe. The arts accepted by Adams, Franklin, and Washington, to name only a few, included architecture, furniture design and construction, ship design and building, weaving and spinning, printing, and political speaking and writing. Portrait painting was acceptable since it preserved elements of the history of the young nation, and folk music was praised, as it came directly from the people and was not refined by courtly manners and demands.

Add to the above the religious objections to the arts that had been voiced from well before the fall of Rome on through the Middle Ages and the Renaissance and still being heard loudly proclaimed from the Puritan pulpits. For some, theater, in particular, was seen to be the work of the devil. After all, it broke two of the Ten Commandments. First, it presented lies like truth. (Plato had made the same observation in his *Republic* and had banned "poets" from his idealized Utopia.[4]) By presenting fictional characters to the public as real people, actors committed falsehoods. It was also claimed that actors assumed characters' often sinful and despicable natures. Since actors often showed characters of questionable morals on stage, it was reasoned, the actors' offstage behavior could not help but be tainted. Second, popular artists and actors were raised above the norm, an undemocratic event, and worshipped by the masses, in violation of the commandment "You shall have no other gods before Me."

Immigrants from England, particularly the Puritans, brought with them the prejudices against practitioners of the theater that had existed in that country for more than 150 years. Dating from the edicts issued against "common players" in the Elizabethan era and on through the passage of the Licensing Act of 1737, actors had been grouped together with other disreputable individuals in the eyes of the law: "rogues, vagabonds, sturdy beggars, and . . . *common players* of interludes."[5]

Echoing the writing of Tertullian[6] (A.D. c.155–c.220), eighteenth-century theologians condemned the theater for "immodesty of gesture," pleasure leading to "spiritual agitation," and "adultery," for, they reasoned, "[The Lord God] regards as adultery all that is unreal." Good Christians, therefore, were prohibited from attending the theater, and in many cases those who were practitioners of the theatrical arts were banned from taking the sacraments. In 1750 guardians of the public good in Boston passed the following ordinance: "To prevent and avoid the many mischiefs which arise from public stage plays, interludes, and other theatrical entertainments, which not only occasion great and unnecessary expense, and discourage industry and frugality, but likewise tend greatly to increase impiety and contempt for religion."[7]

Such attitudes toward the arts and specifically the theater prepared the way for the Continental Congress to ban theater during the American Revolution. Due perhaps to the pleasure George Washington and others found in it, the ban was lifted shortly after the war ended.[8] The negative attitudes toward the theater, however, remained and, to some extent, still are a part of our American culture.

In spite of the opposition outlined above, the theater intrigued many. The first touring player, Anthony Aston, came to the continent and performed in both Charleston and New York in 1703.[9] Since there were no theaters on the North American continent, Aston apparently put on his one-man show in whatever facilities he could find. The first professional company of players, the Murray-Kean Company, arrived in 1749 to find that every colony with the exception of Virginia and Maryland had laws forbidding the staging of plays. Since there were few if any roads, paved or otherwise, and travelers often had to rely on trails, the company found it extremely difficult to tour in such a sparsely inhabited territory. In spite of this, the company succeeded in operating with a degree of profitability and with the support of some freethinking colonial governors, who granted it permission to perform in whatever makeshift facilities were available.

Though the theater was opposed by the clergy and some politicians, audiences found that this art form provided them with an emotional outlet, with an education by example, with commentaries on current leaders and events when it dared, and with an escape from the everyday world into one of the imagination. Gilbert Seldes, critic and commentator on the arts in America, says that the "great arts" have these functions:

They give form and meaning to life, which otherwise might seem shapeless and without sense.

They give us a deeper understanding of our own lives and the lives of others.

They express the spirit of an age or people.

By all these things they create a certain unity of feeling.

They provide diversion from the cares of the day and satisfy desires unfulfilled in our common life.[10]

As it did during the colonial period, during the latter part of the eighteenth century and throughout the nineteenth century the theater brought the outside world into the lives of America's frontiersmen and women. It brought them together as a community. It brought to them views of life in the world as it may or may not have existed well removed from their own remote and isolated settlements.

Actors, during this early era, relied on riverboats, the horse and buggy, or the horse alone in order to move from one engagement to another. It was not an easy life, nor was it safe, for the dangers of traveling on the frontier were many and varied. The memoirs of Sol Smith and Noah M. Ludlow give graphic accounts of the actors' life on the American frontier.[11]

Much of American theater prior to the Civil War, therefore, depended on the efforts of actors banded together as repertory companies. Until Edwin Booth appeared in *Hamlet* for a run of one hundred consecutive performances, there were no long-run presentations in this country. Actors, therefore, had to be prepared to play several roles in rotation throughout the season. The value of an actor to a company rested not only on his talents but on the number of roles he had mastered and his wardrobe. Since actors provided their own costumes, an actor of any repute carried with him his trunks of period and modern costumes appropriate for the roles he was equipped to play.[12]

An actor of star caliber rarely worked as a permanent member of a repertory company, but toured individually from one company to another as a guest star to perform the roles for which he was famous. Edwin Booth, for instance, with the exception of the period from 1869 to 1873 when he managed his own theater, was not attached to any specific company but toured throughout the country appearing with resident companies as a guest.[13] Edwin Forrest, Booth's chief rival, served with a repertory company during the early years of his career, but once stardom had been achieved, appeared only as a guest with resident stock companies throughout the east. When these and other actors of similar stature went to England, the same procedure was followed as they played in London and the Provinces with established repertory companies. Such practices made the life of both the star and the resident company difficult. Often, the star arrived only in time for his performance and had little or no time to rehearse with the company. The result was that actors worked on the basis of tradition. It was readily understood that the star would always have the center position when on stage, and that under no circumstances would a member of the resident company block the view of the audience from the star or upstage him at any time. The idea of having an ensemble of actors on stage, which would be advocated by Constantine Stanislavski in the 1890s, was not accepted by nineteenth-century actors and was often ignored by stars in the twentieth century, with the notable exception of Minnie Maddern Fiske. An additional problem arose when the star had his own cuttings of the plays in which he would appear. It was rare, for instance, for Shakespeare to be presented as originally written. There were as many versions of his plays as there were actors performing them. Resident companies were expected to adapt to whatever version the star used.

The concept of putting together a company of actors specifically chosen and rehearsed for a particular play was introduced to the American theater by playwright-actor-manager Dion Boucicault when he mounted his production of *The Octoroon* in 1859. For this play, Boucicault engaged his actors for an entire season, for it was his plan to tour his complete production once it had exhausted its audience potential in New York City. Part of the reason for this approach lay in the fact that only by keeping his company alive and performing *The Octoroon* could he protect his rights to the play. If he were to abandon the play after its initial run, others could pirate it by changing the title, for the copyright laws in effect prior to 1906 protected only the title of the play not the text. In addition, the rail lines along the East Coast were well established; and Boucicault could move his company, costumes, props, and sets with a degree of efficiency not possible earlier.

Boucicault's plan was successful and spelled the gradual demise of the resident repertory companies throughout the country. By the end of the century a few of the major cities could boast resident stock companies, but repertory companies relying on the talents of visiting stars were rare.

Following the Civil War, a nationwide railway system rapidly developed. Though much had been done prior to the war, the growth of the system had been stemmed by the hostilities. In 1867, 2,541 additional miles of track were completed; and in 1869, 4,103 additional miles were placed in service with the major achievement being the final linking of the Union Pacific and the Central Pacific. This gave the country its first fully operable transcontinental rail line[14] and made possible the establishment of several touring circuits throughout the country. One of the major circuits started in New York, went to Albany, Buffalo, Detroit, Chicago, Milwaukee, Helena, Spokane, Seattle, Portland, San Francisco, and ended in Los Angeles. Other circuits were developed covering the central United States, the South, and the East Coast. Managers attempted to book their productions as economically as possible so their companies would not be forced to backtrack and then leapfrog past previously served markets. Local exhibitors attempted to fill their theaters nightly from September to early May. Since local exhibitors usually contracted to pay the touring companies a percentage of the box office, managers bargained avidly to obtain the most advantageous split possible.

The problems of scheduling such bookings were myriad and were compounded by floods, blizzards, theater fires, and similar disasters. Those and related problems gave rise in 1896 to the establishment of the Theatre Syndicate, also known as the Klaw and Erlanger Syndicate named after the booking agents and theater owners Marc Klaw and Abe Erlanger. The syndicate aimed to provide booking services to both producers and exhibitors.

Up until the time of the syndicate, the booking of touring productions had been handled in a haphazard manner. Managers from the East to the West Coast and from points in between descended on New York during June, July, and August in order to find traveling attractions with which they could fill their theaters during the coming season. Though some major producers established their own booking offices, their total product could hardly fill a season's bookings. In taverns, on street corners, anywhere in the city that theatrical people gathered, local managers sought out independent producers in order to fill the country's theaters for the coming season. Often a touring manager booked a complete season even before beginning to produce his plays. Thus, he was assured of housing his productions. The local exhibitors, however, often had little knowledge of the productions they would finally receive and even less knowledge of the quality of those productions.

Few theater managers cared to risk their time and the reputation of their houses on the untried; therefore, the young producing manager without a reputation had difficulty finding houses for his show. The neophyte often had to locate such bookings as were available and fill them as best he could. This often meant that his company would be faced with the necessity of traveling erratically about the country, frequently doubling back on the route in order to meet commitments. More often, he found after venturing forth that he could not pay the expenses of his travels and that he would have to either turn back or disband the company midroute. This not only placed him on the verge of bankruptcy but destroyed his reputation with exhibitors as well as with the actors who were sometimes stranded in the hinterlands of the country with no funds to return to their home base, New York City. Local exhibitors, of course, were left with no attractions and with dark houses.

The problems faced by producers and by exhibitors were such that the idea of a central booking office appeared to be the ideal solution. Klaw and Erlanger established such an office and secured agreements with the producers represented that they would book exclusively with the newly formed syndicate. Theaters that obtained their shows from Klaw and Erlanger were forced to sign an agreement stating that only with the permission of the syndicate would they book from any other source. The syndicate gave no such permission; and since, with a few exceptions, it booked the best productions available from the most reputable producers, local exhibitors could not afford to breach the agreement. By 1905, the syndicate had control of every first-class theater in the United States. Within another two years, well over 90 percent of the theaters suitable for major touring productions were under the control of the syndicate.[15]

Independent producers and stars were forced to play wherever and whenever they could and under whatever circumstances existed. Leading actress Minnie Maddern Fiske gave readings in the town hall in Salt Lake City when she could not find a theater for her company. Sarah Bernhardt, the famous French actress, performed in a tent in 1906 as she toured the country performing scenes from her most famous plays. She also found local armories in large cities could be adapted to her needs. Director/producer David Belasco, whose productions were the most popular New York City offerings during the first decade of this century, found himself and his companies closed out of the major markets by the syndicate.

Of course, small-town opera houses were of little interest to the syndicate since they were usually too small and too ill equipped to house the productions the syndicate booked. The result was that the small communities, many with populations numbering only in the hundreds, could not see the work of America's major actors and actresses.

During the first decade of the twentieth century, metropolitan areas usually had several theaters presenting regular performances of the major commercial plays of the time. These theaters were classed according to the quality of the productions they offered. "First-class" theaters presented fully mounted productions with experienced casts headed by actors who had become well established as stars. The productions were often duplicates of the plays, musicals, operas, and operettas seen on the New York stage with the same settings, costumes, and casts. Admission might run as high as $2.50 per seat. These theaters were patronized by the wealthier and perhaps better educated citizens of the community.

"Second-class" or "popularly priced" theaters offered much the same fare, but the companies did not have casts of a caliber equal to those seen in the first-class theaters, and the productions were often remountings without stars of presentations that had toured as first-class fare during previous years. The admission price could be as high as $1.50 per seat.

In most cases, first- and second-class theaters offered two different productions per week during the season, which ran from September to early May. The presentation of such productions was possible because of the existence of the railroads, which could transport the casts and the sets both efficiently and rapidly. By the end of the nineteenth century, in an attempt to encourage passenger as well as freight business, the railroads arranged special prices for the touring companies granting them free boxcars for scenery, props, and costumes if a specified number of tickets were purchased. The rail lines also agreed to carry the special cars provided by managers for stars. In some cases, the arrangement included sidetracking the cars carrying the company, stars, and so forth and allowing the company to make use of the facilities as living quarters during a stopover for performances, thus saving the cost of hotel rooms for the actors and crews. By 1920, however, such arrangements had all but disappeared as the railroads came under the jurisdiction of the Interstate Commerce Commission, which discouraged such preferential pricing. The economic impact of this change in touring costs reduced the number of companies on the road and available to local theaters, many of which turned to the exhibition of the feature-length motion pictures that had become available.

In addition to the first- and second-class theaters, a metropolitan area might also have a resident stock company offering a new play weekly. Such plays were often the same as those that had been toured previously and had proved to be successful on the New York stage, though there were exceptions depending on the community and surrounding area. Local managers were well aware of the tastes of their audiences and catered to them as much as possible. The stock company was normally composed of nine to twelve actors, each playing his or her own "line of business"—that is, a specified character type such as leading lady, leading man, heavy, second woman. In addition, the company also had a support staff of stage carpenters, electricians, and others. The actors performing in these theaters were usually relatively young, and the companies provided an important training ground for aspiring thespians.[16] Whereas the best of these companies mounted each play specifically, smaller and less lucrative organizations relied heavily upon stock settings that could be adapted to any of the plays being presented. The companies catered to the middle class and were family oriented with admission prices as low as twenty-five cents for a Saturday matinee.

Only in the largest cities did the fourth form of theater exist. It was usually called the "dime melodrama." Admission was ten cents, and the plays were mounted inexpensively, relying on sensational plots with good pitted against evil in the most elementary of situations. Both in price and content these theaters appealed particularly to blue-collar workers with a minimal educational background.

While large cities might boast such a collection of live theater offerings, small communities could not. They were forced to rely on small touring groups, often of dubious quality and reputation, which played wherever they could find a suitable place—perhaps a barn, the town or Grange hall, or a schoolhouse. Such groups, sometimes called "barnstormers," rarely had more than six people in the entire company, which was often composed of family members. The settings they used were made up of diamond dye drops[17] and legs that could easily be folded and packed in a trunk for moving.

These companies employed the services of an advance man who arranged for a space for a performance and posted notices throughout the community. Unfortunately, a number of these companies reinforced the popular notion of the morals of theater people and earned for themselves the sobriquet "wildcat company." The name suited, for the wildcat would strike rapidly and viciously at its prey. "Wildcat" companies did the same with regard to the communities in which they performed. Such companies often "pirated" their scripts. That is, they used copyrighted material without permission and paid no royalties. In order to avoid detection, they often changed the name of the play and of

INTRODUCTION

the characters. In some cases they advertised to a community the presentation of two evenings of performances with a different play being presented each evening when in reality the same play was being offered under a different title with newly christened characters. On the second evening, at the end of the first act. the company manager, as usual, would collect the box-office receipts and, while the audience was being entertained with an interlude, would join the company backstage to assist in the final actions of packing and loading the costumes and scenery in their touring wagon. The intermission over, the audience awaited the beginning of the second act only to find that the company had disappeared into the night "like a wildcat" having swindled them as well as local merchants and boardinghouses.

Such companies only reinforced the prejudices of audiences that had historically doubted the morality of actors in general. Obviously, the "wildcat company" that behaved in this manner could not expect to be accepted favorably if it were to return to the community it had cheated. Other such companies, as honest as they might be, suffered because of the few and were often invited to leave a town before any performances could be scheduled. If, however, a company's manager were known to be honest and had established a rapport with the community, he and his actors would be welcomed with open arms. Such apparently was the case for Arthur Names and his "Famous Players." Without their reputation as an honest company, they would have suffered the fate of others whose image had been tarnished by the actions of the dishonest.

It was in the very small communities that the Names organization performed; but since Names carried his own performance facilities with him, he was able to mount a better and more thoroughly prepared production than could the "barnstormers" who attempted to perform wherever an audience could be assembled.

McCracken, Kansas, originally the home base for Names, was and still is a very small town on the northwestern edge of Rush County. The county had a total population of 8,360 in 1920.[18] (The towns in the county were so small that the United States Census for 1920 only recorded the county population.) The only north-south "highway" going through McCracken remained unpaved until the early 1960s though the one road running east-west, which followed the Missouri-Pacific railroad line, was paved during the early 1920s. Other roads in the county were little more than wagon trails and still remain mostly unpaved today. McCracken, like most of the other Kansas communities, had electricity fairly early in the century, but the county populace living on farms relied on kerosene and gas lanterns or Delco systems[19] until after World War II, when the efforts of the Rural Electrification Administration, established in 1935, were finally implemented. Still, McCracken was a stop on the Missouri Pacific rail line, a fact that undoubtedly encouraged the community to construct an opera house. Unfortunately the Missouri Pacific did not serve many, if any, large communities. Nor did it terminate at a city large enough to encourage major touring companies to make use of it.

The second home base for Names came in the late 1930s when he joined forces with William A. Whisenhunt in Meadow, Texas. Meadow is a small community in the northeastern corner of Terry County in northwest Texas. In 1940, Meadow had a population of 408 while Terry County's population was 11,160.[20] Meadow was also served by rail, the South Plains and Santa Fe Railroads. Again, it was too small to attract companies touring by that means of transportation. Both towns and others like them could attract only the smallest and least expensive of companies.

In towns such as McCracken and Meadow, the audiences were very limited in size. A company therefore needed several plays in its repertoire in order to attract audiences for more than one performance. Even in larger cities, the first- and second-class theaters booked what were called split-week engagements: one production would be performed Monday through Wednesday with a Wednesday matinee and a second production would fill out the week. Only when the production was so noted that it could draw audiences from many miles around could it be expected to play for an entire week. Such was the case with *Ben Hur* starring William Farnum. This was extremely rare, however, and the only other exception to the split-week scheduling would occur when a company came with a repertoire of plays for a full week's engagement. A good example of such was the company headed by E. H. Southern and Julia Marlowe with their Shakespearean repertoire.

Because communities in which the tent and "barnstormer" companies performed were small, the actions of the performers both on and off stage readily became public knowledge, and the public would not tolerate "visitors" who ignored the local moral codes. As a result, the players, of necessity, kept to themselves for the most part. All evidence indicates that the gregarious Names's behavior within a community was above reproach. It should also be noted that his company did not perform on Sundays. Whether or not they performed on Wednesday evenings, often a church night in the small towns,

INTRODUCTION

is not noted, though to lose one more night's box office would have placed an intolerable financial restriction on a company that often lived hand-to-mouth.

In the smallest of towns, Names's person-to-person approach would be appreciated and the offerings of his company attractive. The theater (tent) became a meeting place for such farm communities, a place where the population could escape its daily battles with the insects and the vagaries of nature that threatened its livelihood, a place where the citizens could share together at least a brief time of relaxation and escape. Along with the church, the theater became a place for social meetings and provided an alternative to the isolation of farm life.

If the behavior of actors was of importance to the reputation and therefore the financial well being of a touring company performing in small communities, of equal importance were the plays that the companies presented. Though the 1920s and 30s were possibly the Golden Age of the American theater with some of America's most accomplished playwrights at work, there is no indication that Names offered the results of their efforts to his audiences. It is probably just as well that he did not.

This was the era of Eugene O'Neill, Maxwell Anderson, Sidney Howard, Elmer Rice, Philip Barry, George S. Kaufman, and Moss Hart. Their plays and the subjects within which they were rooted may have played well in large cities with educated and fairly sophisticated audiences, but they would hardly have appealed to audiences in small-town America. This is especially true when speaking of an area populated with Bohemian and German-Austrian descendants, many of whom still spoke their native languages fluently and, to some extent, exclusively.

As in earlier days, serious questions were raised in major population centers regarding the morality of the stage. In New York attempts were made to establish some form of censorship over the stage, for many felt that the taboos of the past were being ignored by the writers of the present. The plays of Ibsen and Shaw were often frowned upon. Two of O'Neill's plays were closed by the authorities, *All God's Chillun Got Wings* and *Desire Under the Elms*, the first because black and white children were seen playing together on stage during the opening scene and the subject matter concerned miscegenation, the second because O'Neill's New England adaptation of Euripides' *Hypollitus* dealt with adultery and incest. *All God's Chillun* was finally allowed to be performed when the first scene was eliminated. The stage manager read that section of the script to the audience. *Desire Under the Elms* was not allowed to reopen until it had been performed before a censorship jury, which found it to have redeeming social values.[21] In spite of the jury's findings, the theater was raided and the actors and crew arrested when the play was performed on tour in Los Angeles.

Sidney Howard's *They Knew What They Wanted* (1925) and Maxwell Anderson and Lawrence Stallings's *What Price Glory?* (1926) dealt with subject matter and employed language that caused many audience members of the 1920s to gasp with surprise and react in some cases with vivid anger. Elmer Rice's experimentations with expressionism and symbolism astonished and puzzled audiences more used to romantic realism in the theater, and Philip Barry's sophistication was representative of a somewhat glib and perhaps cynical city life totally foreign to rural audiences.

Even the plays of the 1930s were such as to raise the eyebrows of conservative theatergoers as they attempted to reveal the seamier side of our American culture, the fate of the poor and the working man, and Jewish family life in New York City.[22]

For rural audiences such plays would be totally foreign in both subject matter and language. Besides, few, if any, audiences go to the theater to be criticized or educated. Audiences normally attend the theater to be entertained. If they learn something in addition, that is an unexpected benefit. If their beliefs are reinforced, they are comfortable within the venue, but if they feel themselves insulted or are alienated by the playwright or the actors, and if they are not entertained, they will leave angry not only with the playwright, actors, and producers but with the institution as a whole.

Theater as a commercial enterprise cannot afford to alienate its source of income. Companies touring to small communities with limited potential audiences could hardly dare to present the most current plays, much less the controversial plays. Managers of such companies had to have a feel for their audiences, knowing what they would respond to and what might alienate them. In this the owners and managers of the tent shows, such as that controlled by Names, were past masters. Names, by becoming a part of almost any community he visited, was able to judge the type and style of play that would most attract and please his potential audience. The fact that his company often prospered and annually returned to many of the same cities reflects the accuracy of his assessment.

Donald W. Whisenhunt states that Names often spoke of his intentions to take his company to New York. One wonders how Names and his actors would have fared had they attempted to perform plays suitable for remote rural audiences for Broadway playgoers accustomed to the master craftsmen serving the New York stage in this period.

Names and his colleagues in the profession faced two major forms of competition. During the first decade of the twentieth century, motion pictures had become a major source of entertainment. With the ten-minute film *The Great Train Robbery* in 1903, Edwin S. Porter showed that cinema could place before an audience storytelling spectacles that were far more realistic than those that could be created in the live theater. His short melodrama, when expanded, soon began to toll the death knell for the melodrama theaters that relied heavily on stage spectacle and placed little emphasis upon literary elements. In 1915, when D. W. Griffith showed with *The Birth of a Nation* the range of spectacle that could be achieved with the film and the emotional power it could elicit (as well as proving that audiences would pay "road-show" prices to view a film), the competition of the cinema with the live stage became an even greater reality.

In addition, the live theater had, as it sometimes does, come close to committing suicide at the end of the first decade of the century: a plethora of touring companies had been fielded in an attempt to break the hold of the syndicate. Many theaters that had been built during that time and devoted only to live presentations found that they had to exhibit motion pictures to survive. With the success of *The Birth of a Nation*, film producers turned to the production of full-length or feature-length films, often based on the very plays that would otherwise have been available only through the auspices of live touring companies. Writing in 1927, historian Alfred L. Bernheim commented on the competition the motion pictures were giving the live theater:

> **The motion picture industry is carrying on a campaign of conquest in which it does not hesitate at anything it can get away with ... It is buying its rival's theatres even where it cannot use them itself. Better to close them up or turn them into banks or clothing stores than let them draw a dollar away from their own cash boxes. Where it cannot buy them it freezes them out by building its own theatre on the lot next door or opposite, so that it can most conspicuously appeal to the pocketbooks of the theatregoers with the reminder of fifty cents against two dollars and a half.**
>
> **... We have already learned of the shrinkage of the number of legit-**

imate houses in almost every section. The theatres did not vanish into thin air—they became picture palaces.[23]

Even the tent shows were not immune to this type of competition. Motion picture managers attempted to have town councils pass ordinances prohibiting tent shows within the city limits. This failing, they advocated establishing licensing fees so exorbitant that the itinerant tent show could not afford to play in the community. If this did not produce the desired results, the managers resorted to leasing all available lots, thus making them unavailable to the tent shows. In addition, a propaganda campaign was waged against the traveling shows asserting that they took money from the community, whereas the motion picture houses spent their money where they made it.[24]

From the introduction of feature-length films until 1927, the live theater could appeal to audiences only because its actors were alive and because of its adept use of dialogue. In 1927, with Warner Brothers' production of *The Jazz Singer*, the cinema revealed that it, too, could effectively make use of words as well as spectacle and could provide a much more elaborate score for its films than could the local theaters with their house orchestras. With the addition of dialogue, the cinema began attracting stage actors and playwrights by offering salaries the theater could not meet.

The result of this competition from the film industry and the slow demise of profitable touring venues for major productions actually served as a stimulus to the tent shows during the 1920s. Some increased the scope of their offerings by creating a carnival-like atmosphere with game and sideshow tents in addition to the dramatic attraction.[25] Tent-show performers may well have found this venue an improvement compared with some of the theaters in which they had previously performed. Many of the small-town opera houses were notably ill-equipped with small and unheated dressing rooms, slop jars and a pitcher of water in lieu of toilet facilities, and cramped backstages.

Developed during the Industrial Revolution, the cinema was essentially labor efficient. The live theater from its beginnings was labor intensive with the actors and their supporting crews on hand and on payroll for each and every performance. Once a film had been made, it could be shown repeatedly at little or no further cost. Therefore, on an economic basis, the live theater and its practitioners could not compete in any way with the cinema.

In the 1920s a second form of entertainment also enticed the public. As early as 1910, Lee DeForest had demonstrated the possibility of broadcasting a live theatrical performance when he experimented with the new medium of radio by broadcasting a Metropolitan Opera performance of *Cavalieria Rusticana* starring Enrico Caruso.[26] By the middle of the 1920s regular broadcasts were being heard throughout the country in major cities, and by the end of that decade even rural areas could access the airways through the use of crystal- or battery-operated radios. Though many initially may have found this medium expensive, the ability to access the outside world proved to be an enticement few could resist. Even the motion-picture industry felt the rising competition from radio and was spurred on to develop workable means of adding synchronized sound to its films.

Together, the motion pictures and radio provided inexpensive sources of entertainment to a broad spectrum of the American public. They did not provide, however, the excitement of the live actors creating before live audiences, nor did they provide the social atmosphere that has always been a part of the live theater.

Had Names lived to continue his work touring to rural areas, he would have found another obstacle—television. Now performances could be brought into the homes of the audience. Initially, also, the performances were live, thus carrying over from the theater some of the spontaneity that the public had always enjoyed. More important, however, was the fact that the entertainment was essentially free and easily accessed once the prospective audience member had made his or her initial investment in the necessary equipment. There were drawbacks, of course. The social aspects of attending live performances, and even to some extent the motion pictures, were absent in television watching. Interpersonal relations with fair-sized groups in an audience situation were no longer possible since most television audiences were and still are restricted to family situations or individual viewing.

Today many potential audience members remain insulated from the outside world in their homes when not at work. Their behavior patterns are influenced by the scheduling of programs, the manner in which programs are presented, and the fact that how they respond makes little or no difference to those around them or to the performers. For the most part television brings individual experiences to the audience, whereas the live theater depends upon a group experience for its effectiveness. When faced with a social situation in a public setting such as the live theater or cinema, audiences' ingrained behavior patterns become readily evident. Trained to have an attention span of often less than ten minutes because of the interruption of television dramas by commercials, audiences find it a physical, emotional, and intellectual strain to view with little interruption a performance of two or more hours. Personal conversations and physical restlessness often vie with the voices coming from the screen or the stage.

For the performers, far more money may be made by acting in films or performing on television than by acting on stage. Few major stars today will submit to the long hours of travel, the inadequate facilities, and the sometimes difficult living conditions they encounter on the road when lucrative film and television contracts are available to them. The result is that the touring companies that are available often suffer from second- and third-rate casts, poor direction, and inadequate scenic elements. In addition, the fees charged for these companies are so exorbitant that only large theaters and those with subsidies can afford to book them.

In spite of the increased competition the live theater has faced during the twentieth century, it still lives and performs the functions Gilbert Seldes outlined for the arts half a century ago. Though small companies such as the one discussed in this book have disappeared from the scene, they have been replaced by university, college, and high school productions as well as by a variety of community theaters.

Even in the rural areas of the country where current economics makes impossible the support of large or small touring groups, the desire for entertainment lives. As in the past, it is at least partially satisfied through school and church performances. In a few isolated cases, supported by state and federal arts grants or commercial patrons, professional companies still roam the hinterlands performing wherever and whenever they can find a place, the time, and the audience. Training for aspiring actors, no longer available through stock companies and touring companies, has now been taken over by colleges and universities throughout the country.

ONE

An Unlikely Partnership

DUSK IS FALLING, AND ANTICIPATION IS IN THE AIR. ART NAMES has come back to town with his live stage show. Several years have passed since he was here last, and some people in the community wondered if he would ever return.

The tent is on the vacant lot where it has always stood. The weeds have been cut, and the tent has been erected with the help of the men and boys of the town. Now it is opening night, the lights are on outside the tent, and the actors are getting into makeup and costumes. Art Names is dressing in his tuxedo in preparation for his first appearance before the footlights, where he will welcome his old friends from the community and recite a poem in his inimitable style.

Times have changed a great deal since Names first came to town. The country is now engaged in a world war, the second in this century. Many of the young men—and some women—of the town are not here for the show because they are in the military, scattered across the world. Names and his partner each has a son who will soon join them in uniform.

Art Names is well known throughout the region since he has played this area with his tent show since the early 1920s. Many people know him personally and think of him almost as family. His show has few of the characteristics that make other traveling shows suspect in the small towns of America. Art Names is just "regular folks."

During most of his career, Names has operated alone, but because of the hard times of the past decade he has had to bring someone else into his operation. His new partner is William A. Whisenhunt from Meadow, Texas. The partnership of Arthur A. Names and William A. Whisenhunt was most unlikely. Observers would never assume that two men with such different backgrounds would have anything in common, much less that they could enter into a business partnership that involved members of both families and be successful for a period of several years.

Arthur Names was from Kansas. He was better educated than the average person, having attended the University of Kansas and the law school at Washburn University in Topeka. He taught school for about two years, from 1913 to 1915, and served in city government positions in his hometown of McCracken, Kansas, for a period. He was always interested in the theater and often produced plays for his hometown. During World War I he was a pilot and a flight instructor. After World War I he came back to Kansas and continued his involvement in the theater. He provided live stage shows in high school and city auditoriums and finally opened his own tent theater—tent repertory. Names was something of a philosopher and a dreamer as well as a poet and playwright.

Whisenhunt, who was about four years younger than Names, had a much different personal history. He was born in East Texas but had lived most of his early life in central Oklahoma. He went only to about the eighth grade in country schools and had no trade or skill that would distinguish him. He had lived the life of a sharecropper's son in Oklahoma until 1917 when he entered World War I, as did his older brother. He was injured in France in a noncombat accident and remained slightly disabled the rest of his life. His brother was killed in the war, a fact that contributed to his lifelong opposition to war.

Whisenhunt was not as introspective as Names. He was not as well educated and did not read much other than the newspaper to keep up on current affairs. He did not read poetry and may never have seen a live stage performance before Names began to bring his show to his hometown of Meadow, Texas. Whisenhunt was very concerned with making a living and dealing with the world as he met it.

He married in the 1920s and soon had a family of three sons; a fourth son was added in the late 1930s. He had struggled to make a living for his family at various unskilled jobs and had been self-employed on a few occasions, operating a gasoline station and sometimes a billiard parlor. In 1929 he took his family to West Texas; then, after a short return to Oklahoma, he brought his wife and children back to the small town of Meadow, where they stayed for the rest of his life. During the Depression, he had been on relief, but toward the end of the 1930s he was more successful and was able to open another billiard parlor—a pool hall—which he was running when he first met Art Names.

Art Names's tent show had been very successful in the 1920s, but with the Depression the enterprise had suffered. He had to reduce the size of his company and let his actors go. Then in the late 1930s his marriage disintegrated

UNLIKELY PARTNERSHIP

and he was left alone. He was reduced to showing motion pictures in his tent. He was at rock bottom.

Names had begun to play the town of Meadow during the 1920s and became acquainted with Whisenhunt. They seemed to hit it off from the beginning. Names had a lot of time on his hands during the day, and Whisenhunt ran a pool hall where he too had a fair amount of free time.

The two men seemed to be very different, but there were some similarities. They were close to the same age and both came from rural plains states where agricultural radicalism had been important at the time of their births. Names was born in Kansas in 1891 just as the Populist movement was developing into a national party. Whisenhunt was born in Northeast Texas in 1895 and moved to Oklahoma in 1907. Both of them grew up in a time and place of unrest among farmers and the poor. They both had served in World War I, even though they were in different units and probably would not have been friends if they had known one another.

In their adult years, both were suspicious of authority and antagonistic toward men of wealth. Both talked frequently about the "common man" at a time when the common man was suffering from the Depression and when the government of Franklin D. Roosevelt was trying to help the average person. Roosevelt had, in fact, talked about the "forgotten man" in his presidential campaign in 1932.

The men had another thing in common: they were both survivors. Despite adversity, they seemed to persevere. Names's experiences would have destroyed a lesser man. During his traveling days his tent had burned out two or three times, floods had destroyed him, and tornadoes were a constant threat. His marriage had failed, and his wife had left and taken the three children. Sometimes his receipts from the motion pictures were not enough to pay the electric bill.

Whisenhunt bounced from one thing to another. He had no trade or skill and was never a farmer as many people of his background were. He had been a laborer at various times, and for a time he had even tried trapping animals for their fur. When he came back from World War I and could find nothing to do, he and a friend went on the road, hitchhiking and riding the rails. Later, when he was married, he was destitute enough that he had to go on relief on various New Deal programs. Yet he always seemed to bounce back. Clearly, both men were survivors.

Both men were also risk takers. Names may have taken risks because he liked the challenge and did not want to be tied to a routine and boring job.

Whisenhunt, on the other hand, had a family to support without any market-able skills at a time in American history when men of talent, training, and experience were on relief. He had no choice; he had to take risks to survive.

That Whisenhunt would decide to become a partner in a traveling tent show was totally out of character for him. This was a business that put him at risk in a way he had never been before. Even more incredible, he had no experience as a showman. Yet he was never afraid to take a chance. Some-times that meant he failed, but it also meant that he sometimes succeeded where other men would have failed.

That Names would bring a rank amateur into his operation seems odd at first glance. He had been in show business for at least twenty years, and he had worked with some of the best-known tent repertory people in the country. He had been at the top in the middle of the Roaring Twenties. Now he was willing to bring a man into his operation who not only was so different from him but also knew nothing about show business.

Probably the times more than anything else made this unlikely partnership possible. As the Depression waned and war began in Europe, the American economy showed signs of life. Unemployment was declining, farm prices were improving slightly, and the future looked brighter. If the United States were to enter the European war that began in 1939, then the economy probably would boom. Names wanted to take advantage of the new opportunity, and he began to talk to Whisenhunt about getting his stage show back in operation.

Whisenhunt's oldest son was particularly interested and traveled with Names while Whisenhunt continued to operate his pool hall. When America entered World War II, county officials in Terry County, Texas, closed down Whisenhunt's business because of its ambiguous legal status in Texas and because a pool hall, they said, was harmful to the war effort. Whisenhunt now found himself without work, but he did have a small amount of money in savings. Names wanted the show back on the road the way it had been during his good years. One thing led to another, and Whisenhunt contributed his money and became a partner.

The live stage show went back on the road. Even though it lacked the splendor and glitz of earlier years, it was the best that Names could put to-gether with the funds he had. When the show began to play towns where Names was remembered, people turned out to see their old friend.

The Names-Whisenhunt partnership represents a major form of America entertainment that was near its end just as the partnership was formed. The tent show, although little known today, was an important form of entertainment for rural America—particularly since the population of the United States had a rural majority before 1920. Many factors contributed to the tent show's decline, but for Names the Great Depression of the 1930s presented the greatest challenge. Even though this form of entertainment survived World War II only as a shadow of it former glory, it had served its purpose to entertain rural America—and Names was one of its most representative practitioners.

Both Names and Whisenhunt were men who believed in the American dream and pursued it vigorously—even though they did it in very different ways in the years before they joined together. Names, clearly, was interested in the theater from childhood. Until he was about thirty years old, he seemed undecided about a career, probably because of family expectations and his own feeling that he should choose a stable way of making a living. Names was more educated than many of his contemporaries and certainly could have received more education had he so desired. Names had a dream that took him in a different direction. He loved to perform and entertain the public. His eventual decision to make the theater his vocation is merely an example of how Americans have been free to do as they please and to achieve to the best of their abilities—the American dream. Though he lacked the stable background and education that Names had, Whisenhunt wanted to have a family, to support that family, and to rise above the economic and social level of his parents—another American dream.

The fact that these two men came together near the end of both their lives was purely accidental. Yet it seems serendipitous that they should join together at the end of the nation's greatest Depression to improve their financial condition through entertaining.

TWO

Repertoire Tent Theater in America

ART NAMES BECAME A TENT SHOWMAN A FEW YEARS AFTER TENT theater had reached its peak. During World War I, theaters in tents had gone through a major transition, especially from traveling by rail to motorized vehicles. At the beginning of the 1920s, American farmers were doing better than they had for many years, but even after the farm prosperity evaporated in the early 1920s, rural people were still willing to spend some of their small income for familiar entertainment in the form of wholesome, family-type shows. The operators of tent shows continued to prosper through the twenties, and the number of shows on the road increased. With the onset of the Great Depression, the heyday of tent repertoire was over. Shows folded in great numbers. A few survived the difficulties of World War II—rationing, the shortage of actors, the increasing competition of motion pictures—but their days were numbered.

Art Names was able to survive the Great Depression and to reinvent his company during the war years, mostly with the financial assistance and the family participation of the Whisenhunts. Names did not live into the postwar era, so no one knows if he would have been able to carry on beyond the early 1940s. Although Names was not among the most successful of the tent entrepreneurs, his survival instinct and longevity suggest that he might have been able to buck the odds and keep the tent show alive into the postwar era. But the long-term survival of theater under canvas was not to be. This form of entertainment had lived a long life, and new technology and newer forms of entertainment were now replacing it.[1]

Tent theater appeared in the late nineteenth century when theater went on the road, mostly in the summer in the rural areas of America. Repertoire tent shows grew rapidly after 1900 and by 1920 could no longer be ignored as a part of the American entertainment industry. According to William Slout, a historian of tent repertoire: "Development was interwoven with many of the popular amusements of the early century until, carrying the traits and the scars of such diversions as the circus, moving pictures, vaudeville, Chautauqua, and touring opera house companies, the repertoire tent show emerged as a distinct form of rural theatrics."[2]

Tent repertoire evolved most directly from the age of the opera house. Opera houses developed across the country as railroads spanned the continent, and nearly every town of even modest size on major railways had a building to house traveling theater. The name "opera house" was chosen consciously with an eye toward pretension in order to give the theater respectability—something it lacked in America. The reputation of theater and its practitioners—actors—had always been suspect in America. To call the building an opera house—or, as it was sometimes called, academy of music—meant that it was of a "higher class" than the rude entertainment provided in regular theaters.

Opera houses often were owned by the cities in which they were located, sometimes built by public subscription and sometimes with tax funds. These theaters often were pretentious and things of beauty, but, unfortunately, they were not always operated by professionals and were poorly managed. Opera houses also were not always well maintained, a fact that caused traveling companies to endure hardships they would never face in large cities. Theaters often were hot or cold, depending on the season, and the seating and general comfort left much to be desired.[3]

Many small-town opera houses were unable to operate at full capacity, for any number of reasons. Since many were in small towns, they could not attract first-rate companies. Conditions of the theaters—"small, dirty, either too cold or too hot, ill-run, and often unprofitable"[4]—sometimes made them burdens on the community. To fill out their seasons and to provide some income, the theater managers began to turn to the small repertoire companies that traveled the hinterlands. The quality of their productions might be questionable, but most of them could provide one or two weeks of plays without repeating themselves and their small admission prices could attract rural audiences. Even if the limited income did not provide profits for the opera houses, it did provide enough to maintain the theaters.

The development of opera houses spurred the development of repertoire companies to serve them. Tent repertoire companies were descendants of strolling bands that date back at least as far as Shakespeare and were quite similar to the traveling American troupes at the beginning of the twentieth century. They left debt behind them, played tricks on their host communities, and were looked down upon by the people they entertained. Yet they took the theater of London to the countryside and entertained the people. Eventually, they took the theater across the Atlantic to the American colonies.[5]

As America developed and expanded westward, actors organized troupes and went west with the settlers. Even in the hardest of times and most difficult environments, people still wanted to be entertained. By about the 1880s, dramatic touring companies were small groups of actors who could perform plays for at least a week without repeating themselves and who would entertain wherever they went for admission prices of ten, twenty, and thirty cents.

Dramatic repertoire most of the time was a weeklong operation. Sometimes a company might have enough plays to stay two weeks in a community if the business warranted. Selection of plays was determined by the size of the company. Actors often played more than one part, but most companies were too small to perform plays with large casts. Sometimes the owner or actors of the company wrote the plays they performed, but most often they produced plays that were popular in New York or that were old standards and popular in the hinterlands. Seldom did the companies acknowledge the authors or pay royalties. Even though the law was clearly on the side of the playwrights, it was seldom enforced. Company managers regularly changed the names of plays to hide their piracy, to appeal to the audiences, and to trick audiences when they wanted to perform a play that the audience had seen before.[6]

Repertoire companies usually provided vaudeville entertainment between acts of the plays. This allowed time for scenery changes behind the curtain and for companies to make much of their income through selling food and trinkets. The vaudeville acts kept the people in their seats so that sales pitches could be interspersed and more money could be made. Many repertoire companies featured bands that played popular music of the day and music well known in the rural areas. A band concert often preceded the production and served to attract an audience for the play, much the same way as the circus might use a parade to announce its entrance into a community. When a traveling company entered a small town, a marching band attracted attention and advertised the shows to be performed.[7]

In the period after the Civil War until about the end of the century, repertoire companies played in opera houses where they could get bookings. Sometimes these towns were on major rail lines, but many times they were more remote and required repertoire companies to use other forms of transportation. The companies played with fewer actors, had less spectacular equipment and sets, and were looked upon with disfavor in many of the communities where they played. Because of salary costs of outside actors, some companies were composed of a single family, including uncles, aunts, and cousins. As children grew they moved from one type of role to another. By sharing the income among family members, some of whom did not receive a regular salary, some of the marginal companies were able to continue to operate when the economics of their companies would not suggest they could be successful.

By the end of the nineteenth and beginning of the twentieth centuries, road companies were on the decline. Salaries and operating costs were increasing; railroads were charging higher fares and were placing special charges for handling material such as theatrical equipment. Theater managers were becoming more demanding, even when the opera houses were not adequate or properly maintained. The future of the opera houses and the companies that served them appeared bleak.

At the same time, however, a new phenomenon was developing at the beginning of the century, a growing movement toward outdoor entertainment in the summer months. Traditionally, the summer months were considered undesirable for regular indoor productions, whether in New York or in the hinterlands. Yet, at the beginning of the twentieth century, outdoor production seemed to offer a promise of salvation for repertoire theater.[8]

Outdoor entertainment began in resort areas and amusements parks. Roof garden theaters modeled on the German beer garden became popular in the 1890s in metropolitan areas where there were tall buildings. Concerts were a natural for roof garden clubs. The addition of other acts occurred occasionally, but these clubs were not really adaptable to theatrical productions.

Summer resorts at hotels in mountains or at beaches were a natural for light theatrical entertainment. Not all hotels had facilities, but many of them had ballrooms where makeshift productions could be staged. Amusement parks were growing rapidly as a popular form of entertainment for the masses. This form of amusement did not lend itself so well to theatrical productions, but it did show the value and profitability of outdoor entertainment.

Two forms of outdoor entertainment paved the way for the tent repertoire companies. One was the railway park. In about 1900 riding trolley cars to the end of the line became a fad when people of all classes took advantage of the cheap rides and got out of the city for a breath of fresh air and a change of pace. At the end of the line, parks were developed for the entertainment of the city dwellers. A typical park included a pavilion, a boat dock with boats, restaurants, and maybe a small zoo. The major feature, and the great attraction of most of them, was the theater with large seating that operated in the summer months. Most of these theaters were outdoors with no cover from the weather.

The second form of outdoor theater development was the air dome. The success of the park theaters encouraged entrepreneurs to try outdoor theaters in the downtown areas. If these successful shows could be moved to the city center, or at least close to downtown, patrons would not have to travel so far and the theaters could operate every night rather than just on weekends. This was a short season—probably no more than twenty weeks—because of the weather, so no major investments could be made in the facilities. The typical air dome was a stage covered with a roof and with seating for the audience open to the sky surrounded by a high wooden fence.

The air dome lasted for several years, although just how long is not clear. In 1909 the major theatrical publication, *Billboard,* reported that the air dome was a permanent part of the entertainment scene. This optimism was ill founded; the air dome could not continue to operate as city noises became greater and as the price of real estate in downtown areas increased. The property could be used more profitably for other purposes.[9]

The development of outdoor entertainment was a boon for repertoire troupes, even if it was only a short summer season. Outdoor theaters offered a place for them to play that had not been open to them before, and they went back into the opera houses in the winter, when they could. Repertoire companies were becoming more unwelcome in the opera houses as time passed, especially with the rise of motion pictures. By the first decade of the twentieth century, motion pictures had gained a level of acceptance no one anticipated, and many opera houses were converted to the showing of motion pictures almost exclusively.

The development of theater in a tent was apparently of American origin, but tents have been in use for hundreds of years; the first known tent or canopy was invented about 70 B.C. In America tents were used first by circuses after they left permanent buildings and went on the road. Circus tents were round with canvas sidewalls attached. The tents had the obvious advantage over permanent buildings and air domes of being portable. In addition, shows in tents were not subject to cancellation because of rain or other inclement weather. Moreover, they offered the possibility of operating further into the autumn and could start earlier in the spring because the tents kept out the cold wind and were warmer than outdoor theaters. With the development of adequate portable stoves, they could be heated and used almost all year.

Circus tents were not the most ideal for shows that used a stage since they

REPERTOIRE TENT THEATER

were round to allow for the rings used for circus entertainment. To adapt them for other uses, especially to put in a stage, left large areas of the space under canvas unused. The first design of a rectangular tent with an end for a stage appeared about 1910. Several years passed before repertoire companies used the new tent design because few of them could afford to purchase new tents. Most of them started out with used equipment, most of which had been adapted by someone else, or had to be adapted by them, from the round circus tent. When electricity was made practical and readily available in the early years of the twentieth century, the transition from circus round top to canvas opera house was complete, and the tent resembled an indoor theater as much as possible. By 1920 the evolution of the tent theater was complete and did not change again during the life of tent theater.[10]

The Chautauqua was another American institution that used a tent. In the tradition of the lyceum, which had been popular in antebellum America, the Chautauqua was devoted to programs of education and culture and appealed especially to conservative middle-class values found in rural America. Because show people were held in such low esteem in many communities, Chautauqua tents were brown so that people would quickly recognize that they were not show tents, which often were white.[11]

Touring companies were rare before 1885 and developed slowly thereafter. Most early companies were small operations with small casts that toured mostly in small, out-of-the-way places, had no standing in the theater, and were hardly mentioned in the theatrical press. But after 1900 that began to change as tent shows gained a degree of respect and the number of companies increased. Tent show historian William Slout could not say how many shows were touring during 1900–10, but he estimated that there were well over one hundred.[12] Although tent theaters covered the country, most were in the Midwest. Canvas operations became important enough by 1914 that the magazine *Billboard* devoted an entire page to tent repertoire, an act that made the magazine "the tent showman's Bible and created an awareness of industry activity among tent show personnel."[13] Despite the importance of *Billboard* and its publicity for tent shows, many operators, including Names, never reported their activities to the magazine, probably because they did not want their competition to know what they were doing.

The tent show was a rural institution, by and large. It served small towns off the beaten path that were starved for entertainment. Once motorized transportation became reliable and affordable, tent operators could go to virtually any remote location. Prior to that time, they had been limited to playing along railway lines and were forced to pay the rates demanded by the railroads. With trucks and automobiles, shows could set their own schedules, go where they wanted, and operate with fewer expenses.

The fact that the tent show was a rural institution presents a bit of a conundrum. In the 1880s and 1890s, American agriculture was in a desperate condition, yet tent shows prospered generally. The unrest in the farm belt of the South and Midwest became so intense that a new political movement—the Alliance organizations that evolved into the Populist Party—emerged. Despite the scare the farm movement gave the rest of the country and the established political parties, it failed in its immediate goals. William Jennings Bryan, himself a midwesterner from Nebraska, almost by personal acumen alone, turned the Democratic Party toward a more liberal path and adopted most of the Populist platform. Today, almost all the Populist agenda has become law, but many years were to pass before that happened. With the fusion of the Democrats and Populists and Bryan's loss to McKinley in 1896, the farm movement was over.

In the early years of the twentieth century, farm prosperity returned even though the farmers' political movement had little to do with it. The country emerged about 1897 from the depression of the 1890s and better times returned for most of the country, including for tent shows, which prospered and reached their peak. From about 1900 to 1920 farmers were prosperous and the tent show grew and matured as a form of rural entertainment.

Rural communities were of two minds concerning tent shows. On the one hand, they welcomed the entertainment that could be brought to them even though entertainers—actors and other such "disreputable characters"—often were not welcome in the small towns. In many cases, tent shows faced open hostility, but this was not new since theater had never been respectable. Medicine shows and small circuses often took the money and ran. The morals of the traveling groups were questioned, and there was more than one instance when girls of a community were "wronged" by the itinerants.[14]

Fortunately for the tent shows, their acceptance was enhanced by the good reputation of the Chautauqua when it moved into tents and began touring the country. The Chautauqua movement stressed that it was cultural and educational, and its significance is difficult for most people today to comprehend. Chautauqua week was the major social event of the year, and in 1912 more than a thousand independent operations traveled the country.

Chautauquas provided entertainment in the guise of education and culture. Programs included speeches, dramatic readings, impersonations, and illustrated lectures. Rural audiences wanted the escape from their daily lives with the excitement that drama offered. Chautauquas provided entertainment that was like live theater but without the sets, scenery, costumes, and greasepaint associated in the public mind with "show business."

Chautauqua eventually gave in and began to offer plays—as plays—without apology. In the beginning it offered the classics such as Shakespeare, but gradually Chautauqua moved to presenting contemporary plays that were no different from other theatrical presentations. Without question the acceptance by small-town America of the drama provided by the Chautauqua went a long way toward diminishing the hostility and resentment normally reserved for tent shows.[15]

World War I was a major reason tent repertoire prospered. Wartime government spending put more money into the hands of just about everyone, and tent operators were quick to take advantage. With the continuing movement of tent shows to truck transportation, the World War I era proved to be the high point of tent repertoire in America.

With the farm depression that began soon after the war and lasted until the outbreak of World War II, tent shows suffered. Many went out of business in the 1920s and 1930s, but the Great Depression of the 1930s was, by far, the most significant reason for the decline of tent repertoire.[16]

Arthur Names came into show business when tent repertoire was just beyond its peak of success. He did not move into tents until after 1920 when the shows were on the decline, but he prospered generally throughout the 1920s. His problems came in the Great Depression just as most tent shows declined.

During his heyday, Names was a successful tent show operator. He was never the largest or best known, but where he played he was loved by the audiences and welcomed each year when he came through. His movement into professional theater illuminates tent theater.

THREE

Prairie Origins

ARTHUR NAMES AND WILLIAM WHISENHUNT WERE UNLIKELY candidates to go into show business—and especially to travel around the country with a stage show in a tent. Both of them came from families that were not particularly receptive to a career in entertainment.

Given his background, Names was probably the more logical one, but there was little likelihood that a boy born on the plains of Kansas in 1891 would have dreams and ambitions of writing and producing plays, writing poetry, and even becoming governor of Kansas. Yet these were his dreams.

The details of Art Names's life are sparse. Everyone who knew Names had strong opinions and was anxious to talk about him. Some of the memories provided by people who knew him conflicted or contradicted the stories told by others, or they were placed in time only very generally. During his early years in McCracken, Kansas, Names was often mentioned in the local newspaper, mostly because of his theatrical activities, his teaching, or his involvement in city government. Many people who knew him told similar stories that proved untrue when these and other records were checked. Still, the contradictions do not make much difference to the overall story.

Arthur Andrew Names was born on November 13, 1891, about four miles from Hoisington, Kansas, the son of Andrew Baird and Mary Caroline (Hicks) Names.[1] By the time Names was an adolescent, the family had moved to McCracken, Kansas. His father, who was a farmer and at times ran a creamery, was an alcoholic who could be mean when he was drinking; some relatives were afraid of him and tried to stay out of his way during those times. Apparently the father's behavior had its influence on the son. In later life, Art Names was never known to drink and disapproved of drinking in others.[2] This attitude continued when he had his tent show. He made it clear to his actors that he did not want any drinking, gambling, or profane language, but show business being what it was, he was not always able to prevent these activities.[3]

Art Names's mother, Mary Hicks Names, had been a teacher. She was interested in her son's education and encouraged him when she could; she very much wanted him to go into law and was disappointed when he did not. She was bothered by his interest in the theater and in music, but like many devoted mothers, she supported him in what he chose to do in his adult life.[4] One might assume that she was long-suffering, having a husband who drank, children who died in infancy, and a son who entered a profession not considered respectable by many or financially secure.

Six children were born into the Names family, but only Art and one sister, Violet, lived to adulthood. One of the sons, Johnnie, was dragged to death by his favorite pony at the age of ten. The other three children died of various childhood illnesses. Violet became a pharmacist and eventually settled in Colorado. In the later years of Mary Names's life, she and Violet took a homestead near Chivington and Eads, Colorado.[5] The fact that Art and his sister Violet were the only survivors of the family may have been partially responsible for their closeness in their adult years. During his days of traveling with his show, Art always kept in touch with his sister and wrote her often.[6] When his sister had time off from her job, she sometimes came to the town where the show was playing to visit for a few days.[7]

People who lived in the McCracken area and remembered Names as he was growing up have diverse and sometimes conflicting memories of him. Some remember him as something of a "loner" who was more interested in reading philosophy, history, and poetry and in writing plays and poetry of his own. But he also had a gregarious side and people liked him. Though he may have been a loner and interested in things of the mind, he was always spoken of with fondness by the people who knew him. He seems to have been well liked generally and often was sought for public activities.

Still, the image of his being something of a dreamer persists. For example, his cousin Ruth Stump remembered him as a very studious person who was usually off by himself reading or writing poetry. Sometimes when he was coming down the road in his buggy, his horse "Old Allie" would have his head almost down to the ground and would be barely moving. Stump said, "You could hear Art reciting a poem or he would have his head buried in a book."

Stump said that Art did not like to be bothered when he was reading. She loved to tease him when he was reading, but she usually got the worst of the experience. Once when she was dressed in her Sunday best, she kept pulling his hair until he had had enough. He jumped up, grabbed her, and threw her in the horse tank, good white shoes and good dress notwithstanding.[8]

Names, some said, was merely a dreamer without any ambition or direction. Cleo Akers, who said he grew up with Names, reported that he "knew him as a good hard working boy with a lot of wild ideas and not a real leaning toward anything."[9] As events of his life suggest, he was unable to settle on one thing to do. It seems that his real interest was in the theater and that he tried other things mostly to please his mother.

Friends of Names remembered him in different ways. Fred Ford remembered him as a man riding back and forth to town wearing a handkerchief, with knots tied in the four corners, on his head to protect it from the sun. Later, when he was operating his own traveling show, he could often be found working around the tent with a handkerchief on his head, which by the time he was in his fifties was bald and in need of protection from the hot sun of the prairies. Ford remembered him riding to work in town on a horse carrying his typewriter with him. Whether he used the typewriter for a job he might have or whether he carried it so he would have it if he decided he wanted to write something is not clear.

Art yearned for adventure and would take some risks to find it. In another story, Fred Ford said Art was always trying to get him to go under the railroad bridge near the Names family home when a train passed. Ford finally agreed. He recalled that when they were under the bridge, the hot cinders rolled down his neck from the steam engine as it passed over. Ford said he was afraid, but Art relished this kind of adventure as a young boy.[10]

Another friend, Frank A. Murphy, told of a baseball game in the period around 1901–1903 when the boys were all about ten or twelve years old. Murphy said that his team was from the Hampton community and they were playing the McCracken team. Art Names was the umpire. Someone objected to one of Art's calls, and, to settle the matter, the boys decided on a wrestling match. The country team chose Murphy to wrestle Art. Murphy threw Art and the Hampton team won the game.

Murphy did not see much of Art after that until about 1908. During the wheat harvest, Art was working for another man who had teamed up with Murphy's father. Murphy and Art were together working on the harvester. Murphy believed that Art was going to the University of Kansas at the time, and he brought his college books, papers, and other material to read as he drove along. Murphy remembered that Art did not do very much work, and he believed that Art's employer had hired him so he would have the use of Art's horse for the harvest.

During a lull in the work because of wet wheat, Murphy and Art got into a wrestling match. Murphy believed that Art was trying to settle the score of six or eight years earlier at the baseball game. Murphy said he threw Names again and "we got to be real good friends from there on."[11]

The social and political environment in Kansas must have influenced the boy to some extent. In an atmosphere of agrarian unrest, the Populist Party, which entered national politics in 1892, was causing considerable upheaval in eastern Kansas at the time of Names's birth. The impact on Names is reflected in his later suspicion of "the interests": big business, bankers, financiers.[12] Names probably was aware at the time of one of the most articulate commentators on the Populist movement in Kansas, William Allen White, editor of the *Emporia Gazette*. White, a Republican not sympathetic to the farmers' complaints, won a Pulitzer Prize for an editorial he wrote for his newspaper on the Populists.[13] Names later was a good friend of White, and both were members of the Kansas Authors Club.[14] Names was elected to membership in the organization in 1920 "in recognition of his work as a writer of Kansas plays." The McCracken newspaper said it was an exclusive organization composed of "celebrated Kansas authors." The president of the club, Professor James W. Learson of Manhattan, Kansas, recommended him.[15]

By the time Names was old enough to be conscious of public affairs, the turmoil of the farm protest had subsided. Even so, Kansas retained a tradition of agrarian radicalism. Names's political philosophy, which was expressed more clearly and articulately as an adult, reflects a measure of this rural philosophy. Although tying Names's later political philosophy to the political and social turmoil of his youth is tenuous, one must conclude that there was some influence. The third party influence of the Populists surely had some impact on Names's later rejection of all political parties. His antiwar attitude in the 1930s may have come from his own experiences in World War I, the sensational congressional hearings of the Nye Committee in the 1930s, or the traditional midwestern attitude of isolation. Names was a product of his region, to be sure.

The events of his childhood, teenage years, and early adulthood do not reflect anything unusual as far as his political philosophy is concerned. The limited records available show him to be a typical Kansas boy, except for his interest in the theater. In his early years he seems to have flitted from one thing to another. For a young man without a farm to inherit in a predominantly farming region, this may not have been unusual. He did become interested in politics at a relatively young age.

One of the enduring myths about Names among those who knew him is his education. Many believed he was a graduate of the University of Kansas, had a law degree from Washburn University Law School, and was a practicing attorney. Officials at those institutions can verify none of these claims.

Names apparently graduated from high school in 1907 at the age of fifteen. Records are not available to confirm that he actually graduated from high school, but the McCracken newspaper reported in 1907 that four young people were to leave that week "to enter the Lawrence University," apparently a reference to the University of Kansas, located in Lawrence. Two people other than Art listed as planning to enter the university were Violet Names, Art's sister, and Cora Hicks, possibly a cousin of Art and Violet.[16]

Names apparently attended the University of Kansas for only one year, but it was much later than 1907. According to the assistant registrar at the University of Kansas in 1995, the records of the university show that Arthur Names matriculated on October 18, 1915, and that he attended for only one year, 1915–16. There is no record that he ever returned.[17] There is nothing to indicate that he actually went to Lawrence in 1907. If he attended a college other than the University of Kansas, it cannot be verified. The extent of his college education, therefore, seems to be one year.

The local newspaper reported in December 1912 that Names left McCracken that month to go to Topeka where he entered law school.[18] A search of the records of Washburn University Law School in Topeka shows that he was a first-year law student at Washburn in 1911.[19] A letter from Names dated in 1911 is on the letterhead of a law firm in Lyons, Kansas. No verification is possible of what he was doing at the firm, although he may have been "reading law," a practice common at the time in which an aspiring lawyer worked in a law firm and read the attorney's law books. When he thought he was prepared, the "reader" could sit for the bar exam. In Lyons he may simply have been a law clerk, possibly after his year of law school at Washburn in 1911.[20] The discrepancy in dates cannot be explained. The local newspaper may have reported his plans but never followed up on what he actually did.

After Names returned from World War I the local paper reported in April 1920 that he would be leaving for Topeka where he would finish studying law.[21] Without explanation of the law school issue, the paper reported in June, only two months later, that Names was studying public speaking and dramatic arts at the Horner Institute in Kansas City.[22] As late as 1922 the matter of going to law school was mentioned again when the local paper reported, "Arthur Names is divided in his mind about going to college and completing his law course or getting married. If the latter, he thinks he will get all the law will give him."[23] By this time, Names was more than thirty years of age and apparently still uncertain about his future.

Even so, many people who knew him thought he had graduated from law school. His wife later said that he had finished law school and that "he had a lifetime scholarship to go back any time he wanted." Names may have perpetuated the myth that he was a lawyer, and later his partner Whisenhunt believed he was a lawyer.[24] No evidence has been unearthed showing that Names was ever a lawyer. A review in 1995 of the Roll of Kansas Attorneys from 1910 to 1930 does not show Arthur Names on the list. Moreover, he was not listed among admitted attorneys as found in the Kansas Reports of 1938.[25]

Between 1910 and 1922 the records reveal that Names was doing many different things, some of them for very short periods. For example, in 1910 he was reported to be working as a clerk in the Wilson and Ward clothing store in McCracken[26]; then in 1911 he was writing from the law firm in Lyons.

From an early age, Names was interested in the theater. He started writing plays as a teenager and soon was producing them using local talent, sometimes in the high school auditorium and sometimes in the community opera house. As early as 1912 he acted in a play, *The Tyranny of Gold*, that he had written and directed in the town of LaCrosse.[27] Three weeks later, the local paper reported that Names had gone to Colorado to spend the summer working on a ranch.[28] He may not have gone to Colorado, or if he did, he did not stay long because in July or August he and his cousin, Leonard Ryan, leased the community opera house and began presenting plays. It was sometimes called Art Names' Opera House and sometimes the Ryan Theatre Company. Most of the plays presented seem to have been original plays written by Names. At the end of this year he was reported going to Topeka to enter law school,[29] but it seems clear that he did not enter the study of law. The status of the opera house during the next several months is not clear although he and Ryan apparently kept the theater running while he did other things at the same time.

In July, 1913, Names was granted a teaching certificate.[30] Apparently, he had not gone to college yet, although he had attended law school for one year by this time. To teach without college experience was common at the time; many young people graduated from high school and then began teaching. In

August, in a report on the city schools, the newspaper listed Arthur Names as teaching grammar but did not indicate at what level.[31] One of his former students, Mrs. Frank Sutton, reported that he was her eighth grade teacher. She said that while he was teaching he used the talent of the local high school and performed many plays that he had written.[32] They were probably performed in the opera house he and Ryan had rented, but they may have traveled to neighboring communities as well. Nancy Wilson reported that she performed in Names's plays while she was in high school in McCracken in the period of 1920–23, but Names was using local talent earlier and taking the shows to other communities. Wilson said that she was thrilled to be in his plays but that her strict parents would allow her to perform only at home; she could not travel to other towns with the company.[33] Through these years up until Names entered military service the newspaper regularly reported that new Names plays were being performed in McCracken and other towns.[34]

Names apparently taught school for two years, 1913–14 and 1914–15. The newspaper reported that he was teaching for a second year in McCracken and that a month later he was in a group of people who were in LaCrosse, Kansas, taking the teacher's examination. In January, 1915, he was reported ill with "an attack of grip" and was unable to teach for several days.[35]

While Names was teaching he was also public-spirited and served his community in a variety of ways. In 1914 he was elected vice president of the McCracken Commercial Club,[36] probably similar to today's Chamber of Commerce. In 1915 Names ran for the elected position of police judge of Mc-Cracken, but he came in third in a field of five.[37]

During 1916 and 1917 the Names-Ryan partnership was very active. In June 1916 the two of them put up an air dome in McCracken, probably similar to those described in the previous chapter. The structure would seat more people than the local opera house and was more comfortable in the cooler air. The newspaper report mentioned that the air dome had "two projectors so the shows will run smoother."[38] If they were running motion pictures at this time, they were silent movies, to be sure. By 1917 the Names-Ryan company was cooperating with Helen B. Ross and Joe Sims, a married couple who were well-known repertory show people active in the plains states. Names was later a partner with Sims, but it is not clear if they had a business arrangement this early.[39] In 1917 the Helen B. Ross Company presented a new play by Names, *Bone Dry*, a temperance play showing the evils of alcohol. The subject of the play may have been in part directed at Joe Sims, who played one of the leading roles and who himself had a drinking problem, something that Names could not tolerate. The theme of the play seemed prescient as the movement toward national prohibition was reaching a climax. Part of the plot also had to do with the suffrage movement, which was at its height at the time.[40]

In April, 1917, President Woodrow Wilson asked Congress to declare war on Germany, and America entered what later became known as World War I. This war had been under way in Europe since August, 1914, but Wilson had made every effort to keep the United States out of it. One crisis after another eventually led Wilson to the conclusion that he had no choice but to enter. When Congress declared war, young men began to enlist in large numbers, but eventually a conscription law was necessary.

Names watched the progress of the war and the movement of America toward involvement. His views on war at this point in his life are not known, but like many young men of the era, Names decided to enlist in the army in August, 1917.[41] By September he had received a promotion to section chief at the Medical Officers Training Camp at Fort Riley, Kansas. According to the local paper, he still had his interest in the Names-Ryan Company while he was in the military.[42]

Names had an interest in aeronautics and wanted to fly during the war, though at that time there was no real air force, as such. In fact, the airplane had not been proven as a weapon of war and there were many skeptics who believed it would never be effective. Names was one of the advocates of the airplane. His family liked to tell the story of how he got into pilot training. Names was a small man and there was a minimum height requirement for the army air service. During the physical examination for admission Names was sure he would be rejected because he was too short. He was standing with his back to the wall of the examination room, which had a three-fourths-inch molding around the bottom at the floor. Names put his heels on the molding, stretched to his greatest height, passed the height test, and was admitted to flight training.[43]

He became a trainer for pilots and spent some time in the Puget Sound area of Washington State. Like most outsiders he was impressed, or at least affected, by the rain in Washington State, even writing a poem about it.[44] One of Names's sons told the story of the time when Art was stationed in Bakersfield, California. The commanding officer at the Bakersfield base saw a plane come in for a landing on a wet runway, skidding across the tarmac. Unable to see the pilot, the commander said, "My God, there's a runaway plane." Just then Art stuck his head up.[45]

When Names was discharged is not clear, and military records are not available. In August, 1918, the McCracken paper printed a list of local boys who served in the military, and Names was on it.[46] In November, 1918, the same month as the armistice, Names was elected a city commissioner of Mc-Cracken. There was no mention of when he was discharged or whether he actually was out of the service when elected to this city position.

Though the newspaper report indicates that Names was elected a city commissioner in November, 1918, the minute book of the City of McCracken provides another story that confuses the issue. On April 29, 1919, the city commissioners-elect were called to a special meeting because one of the newly elected members, G. M. Ryan, failed to qualify for the position. The commission declared the position vacant and proceeded to elect Names to fill the position.[47]

Art's career with the city council lasted slightly more than a year. On May 6, 1919, Names was elected chairman of the commission and mayor of Mc-Cracken.[48] Under the commission form of government, which was still relatively new at the time, commissioners elected one of their own as a weak mayor. The commission was unclear about some provisions of the law allowing for the new system since this was the first election under the new law and no provision had been made as to the length of the term of each of the three commissioners. On May 19 Names reported that he had written a letter to the League of Kansas Municipalities to clarify this matter.[49] A week later the commission decided to award the three-year term to the member who had received the most votes, the two-year term to the second highest vote getter, and the one-year term to the person with the third most votes.[50] Names remained as mayor and a member of the commission until July 16, 1920, when he resigned both as mayor and commissioner. No reason was given for the resignation and the minutes of the commission do not indicate that there was any discussion of the request other than approving the resignation and appointing a replacement.[51] This was when Names reported that he was going back to law school but then was reported as attending Horner Institute in Kansas City.

During these years after returning from military service, Names apparently retained his interest in the Names-Ryan partnership and continued to write and produce plays. The records are a bit sparse until 1920 when in September he went to the town of Healy to give a reading and in December was elected to the Kansas Authors Club.[52] During 1921 he introduced two new plays, the first, *Alfalfa Jones*, an agricultural play in which Art played the part of a farmer, was presented at the opera house in February to the largest crowd ever in attendance. In December he presented *Nobody Home,* which the newspaper said was modeled on some of the local citizens of McCracken.[53]

The year 1922 was a busy one for Names. He was still actively associated with Helen B. Ross and Joe Sims, and he and Sims collaborated on a number of plays or rewrites of plays that one or the other of them had done before. Names was still taking his plays to neighboring communities: in January, 1922, for instance, his company performed his play *Nobody Home* in the nearby town of Nekoma, Kansas.[54]

He was also still involved in business in McCracken. In August, 1922, the newspaper reported that he was one of a number of businessmen in Mc-Cracken and was managing the Strand Theater.[55] Three months later the paper reported that Names had bought the Strand Theater and was remodeling it. Names reported, "When it is finished McCracken will have one of the best opera houses between Great Bend and Pueblo." During November he had a "pretty girl" contest with men in women's clothing to attract an audience.[56]

The year 1922 was also important for several other reasons. Names felt it necessary to leave the partnership or whatever arrangement he had with Helen B. Ross and Joe Sims. Sims had a drinking problem, though from all reports he was quite talented. In 1922 or 1923 Names also became associated with Milburn Stone, who became known to almost all Americans as Doc Adams on the long-running television series *Gunsmoke.* Stone was a native of Kansas who got his start with Names.

Stone explained that Names had just ended his association with Sims when they met. Stone became acquainted with Names when he and Sims played his hometown of Burrton. Stone said that he was a rather "wild" young man, and everyone in town, except his mother, wanted him to go with Names to get him out of town. Names liked Stone and agreed that he would hire him for a new company he was creating. Names told Stone he would be back through Burrton on a certain day and that Stone should be ready to go, but when Art came back Stone was not there. He had been to a baseball game in another town and had stayed overnight because he had fallen in love with a girl. When he got home, he was told that Art had come for him. He thought he had missed his opportunity, but he later located Names and an arrangement was made.

Stone said that Sims also offered him a job at fifty dollars per week, a fantastic salary for 1922. Names told Stone he was going to start a three-person company consisting of Names, Stone, and Loraine Smith, a piano player. Stone was tempted by the salary Sims offered him, but the decision was made for him, as Stone said, because "Sims got drunk in the last show with Art, and that convinced me to go with Art."

The Names-Stone relationship lasted about five years. At first, only the three of them—Names, Stone, and Smith—traveled from town to town and played in community opera houses, school auditoriums, or any place Names could find. Sometimes they picked up local talent to fill in for some of the plays, but most of the time the entire show was provided by the three in the company.

Stone told the story of his first night with Names. While playing in Trousdale, Kansas, Names went before the audience between acts and informed the patrons that the next night they would be performing a three-act play called *The Midnight Dawn.* Stone and the rest of the company were dumbfounded since they had never heard of the play. The cast members thought they were in town for only one night; now Names had announced that they would perform a play the next night they had never heard of. Stone said he "went into shock." After the show Names handed him a script. According to Stone it was practically a monologue for the character he would play. The character was a shell-shocked young veteran who went in and out of lucidity. When the character slipped into a trance, he would always say, "It was hell out there, hell out there last night."

Stone said he told Names to his face that he was crazy and asked him how he thought anyone could be ready for a new play in one day. Names told him that he would do it because "anybody can do anything." That made Stone even more furious, but Art persisted. "He just did it to test me to see if I'd turn tail and run," Stone said. Stone did not run, and he loved to tell this story in later years. He said, "I'll never forget this, and I've told the story a million times, and it's true. Now this was my second professional performance." Stone said that any time he got stuck in his dialogue, he would go into the trance and say, "It was hell out there."

When they started, Stone and Names shared a room, and Stone was surprised to discover the first night that he and Names would share the same bed. Stone said, "I got in bed, and before he got in bed he took off all his clothes, every stitch he had on, and he threw the window up clear to the top and knelt down in the window, and was naked as a jaybird praying in that window. I couldn't believe it, could not believe my eyes. When he finished he didn't put the window down at all; he just jumped back in bed as fast as he could and was asleep in two minutes."

During the time he was with Names, Stone married Loraine Smith and they continued to perform together. When they started, they were a company of three people; later in the mid-1920s they had a company of eighteen people, including a band and orchestra. Stone said, "We had a seven-piece band at one time and a big show, a very big show."

Stone often thought of Names as a father figure. He believed that Names loved him like a son and wanted him to be as good as he could be, both on and off the stage. Stone said he was a rather profane, rough-edged country boy who had learned all the lumberjack language in the world and used it all the time. When he began living with Names, it occurred to him that he was swearing all the time and that Names never did. This brought him up short.

Stone said that Names taught him the most important thing he ever learned about acting. Names told him that acting was not the most honorable or the most noble profession, but it was very gratifying. He said you must never let anyone catch you acting, you had to be yourself, be honest when off stage, and not be dishonest with the public. Names told him too many people were always acting. If Stone allowed that to happen, Names said, "Nobody will ever know who the hell you are."[57]

Names was something of a socialist at heart. During the 1920s when the show made a lot of money, Art's wife said that he wanted to share his good fortune with the actors. He set himself a certain level of profit and any income over that he would divide equally among the actors and musicians, but not among the crew. She remembered this with a hint of bitterness, saying, "It was very disastrous. You know most people can't stand prosperity."[58] Names always liked to talk to the company, but the actors did not want to hear a lecture from him. They wanted only to have their bonuses so they could drink and gamble, something Names did not approve of but which he could not control.[59] Stone was still impressed almost fifty years later with Names's generosity. Stone said, "Sometimes it was a feast or famine. Art put in a system of bonuses. We shared the wealth. Everybody shared and shared alike." Once while the show was in Texas, Art came to Stone and told him about his system of bonuses and gave him some money. Names said to Stone, "'This makes you the highest paid actor out of the Kansas City Equity office.' He said, 'You're on your way.'" As best as Stone could recall, he and his wife together were earning something like $275 per week, a fantastic salary for the time.[60]

The most significant event for Names in the early 1920s was meeting the woman who became his wife, Maurine Allen. She was from an old show-business family that had been in vaudeville at first, but her family knew that form of theater was dying. She began on the vaudeville stage when she was eleven years old, but the family soon moved into drama. Maurine believed this was the best move they could have made. The transition was easier because the family had an excellent director and teacher, a man from Florida who taught her all she knew about stage acting.

Maurine Allen met Art Names when she was fourteen. She and her youngest sister were working with a repertory company operated by a woman who had a copy of one of Names's scripts, *That's Where the West Begins*. This was one of Art's most successful plays, and the woman was using it without his consent and without paying him royalty.

When Art's show was playing close to this company's location, he came over to see the woman to "give her hell about using his play." Instead, he met Maurine and was smitten. He asked her employer many questions about her, and he asked if it would be all right if he took Maurine for a ride in his car. He took her to the other town where he was working and introduced her to Milburn Stone and Loraine Smith. Maurine later said that was her first date with Art—and the first date of her life.

Names had a change of heart about the woman using his play. In fact, he worked with her to revise it to fit her cast better. Maybe he was trying to impress Maurine's boss because he was interested in Maurine.

Maurine and her sister finished the season, but then Maurine found herself in an awkward situation. Her mother, who had been ill, died near the end of the season, and then her sister got married. That left Maurine alone. Soon after she met Names, he wrote and asked if she would join his show, alone. He was sensitive to the fact that she was working with her sister and that they both were very young. He did not have a place for the sister, since he wanted to start a four-person company and already had Stone and Smith. When her sister decided to get married, that removed any obstacle to Maurine's joining Names's company.[61] She accepted his offer, and within a few months she and Names were married, in February, 1924.[62] They had their first child, Art Names, Jr., in July, 1925, and on October 2, 1927, they had twin sons, Jack and Jean.[63]

When Maurine joined the show, its nature changed. For one thing, Art renamed the company the Allen Players because he thought her family's name was better known and would be good for business. Later they changed the name to Allen-Names and then the Art Names Players. Through the years, the show operated under a variety of names.[64]

Maurine was about seventeen or eighteen, and Art, at thirty-two, was fifteen or more years older than she was. She left the running of the show to her husband. Though she had been raised in a show-business family, she was shy and reluctant to meet the public and did not mix well with people. She had been told by her family not to try to associate with people in the towns where they played because they would be gone in a few days and, more important, because though the people might come to be entertained they would not accept show people socially. Maurine remembered, "You might as well have associated with someone in the red-light district. It was bad; it was very bad. My grandparents cautioned us, and we were not allowed to discuss our parents and their travels or anything." She had the same attitude when she married Names.[65]

After the marriage, Art's relationship with Stone began to deteriorate because Maurine and Stone had trouble getting along. Part of the problem may have been that Maurine was young and, coming from a show-business family, thought she knew more about acting than Stone did. Stone told about several disagreements with Maurine. When Maurine organized a birthday party for Art, Stone said that his wife did most of the work and that he and his wife contributed more to the party than anyone else. During the party, Maurine made some remarks that highly offended Stone, and he in turn said some things very unflattering about her. When Stone got back to his hotel room, Names came and insisted that he apologize to Maurine, but Stone refused. Names said, "I am going to sleep on it," an expression he used often. That was the last time it was mentioned, but it did create tension between the two friends.[66]

On another occasion, Stone and Maurine had trouble onstage. Stone said she thought of him as a hick and acted superior to him. Once on stage in a scene with her, he jumped a cue, and she blurted out, "Shut up!" right in the middle of the scene. After the show they had a serious argument, and each said things that hurt the other. Stone said he was going to leave the show, but Art talked him out of it. He told Art he would stay if Maurine never said another word to him, except for business.[67]

Their problems likely stemmed from two very high-strung temperaments. In addition, Maurine was immature and Stone was a highly paid actor who probably thought he was better than the kind of show in which he was working. He was already considering trying his luck in New York. He later said that most of his animosity toward Maurine stemmed from the fact that he loved Art so much and did not like what she did to him and the way she treated him.[68]

In 1927 Milburn Stone and his wife left the Names Company. The animosity between Stone and Maurine played a part in the decision, but Stone also had outgrown the rural theater and was ready to try his luck in the big time. He left Names and went with another company, the Harold Davis Show, for a while, then got his courage up and went to New York. At that time, the New York stage was the most prestigious place for an actor and was the mark of success. Hollywood was still in its infancy, and Stone did not consider going there. He made his move to New York just about the time that talking pictures became all the rage. He later said that talking pictures wrecked his trip to New York, and he eventually found himself in Hollywood trying to make it in motion pictures.[69]

The company reached its pinnacle of success just as Stone was leaving. Hard times were just around the corner, although some time passed before they were felt by Names. The Great Depression became the greatest test of Names's professional ability and a severe challenge to his marriage. At this low point in his life, Names became interested in Whisenhunt as a partner.

When Names and Whisenhunt decided to team up, Names had more than twenty years' experience in show business while Whisenhunt had none. In fact, show business was a very unlikely field for William Whisenhunt, a mature man with a family to support. Whisenhunt—commonly called "Bill" by everyone who knew him—would never have thought as a child that he would be a "showman" by the time he was almost fifty years old.[70]

Whisenhunt's background was not distinguished at all. He came from a family that had come to America in the 1730s, but genealogy, family history, and tradition meant very little to him or to the family in which he was raised. In the early history of the family there is evidence that there may have been some modest wealth, but by the time Whisenhunt was born, little was evident. The records show that his grandfather had one thousand dollars' worth of real estate in 1880, but what happened to that land is not clear.[71] When Whisenhunt was born, his father was a sharecropper, and the family just barely got by from day to day.

Whisenhunt was born in the village of Ivanhoe, in Fannin County, Texas, on October 29, 1895, the eighth of eleven children born to George Washington and Missouri Tennessee (Batton) Whisenhunt. Only one of the eleven children died as an infant, a remarkable survival rate among families of that era.

Whisenhunt's father was a hardscrabble sharecropper who had difficulty providing for his large family. Somewhere in his youth he lost one of his eyes, and he always had a rather unbalanced appearance after that. Whisenhunt liked to tell the story of how his father would go fishing and catch a large number of catfish. He would put them in the back of a wagon and go up and down the rural roads trying to sell the fresh fish by yelling as he came to a farmhouse. When a catfish would die without water, he would toss the fish into the ditch to rot.

Fannin County, Texas, is in Northeast Texas with its northern boundary being the Red River. During Whisenhunt's youth, the area across the river was Indian Territory that had been established originally as a permanent home for the various native Indian tribes and those who had been moved there by the government.

Already by the time Whisenhunt was born, Indian Territory was being breached and some of the better land was being carved out for white settlers. In 1907 the transition was complete, and Oklahoma was admitted as a state. In that year, George Whisenhunt picked up all his family, except the oldest child, Lillie, who was married, and moved them across the river into Oklahoma. The family eventually settled in Erin Springs, a small village in Garvin County, Oklahoma, with Lindsay as the nearest town of any size only a few miles away. Why the Whisenhunt family moved to Oklahoma in 1907 is not clear. It may have had something to do with Oklahoma statehood or it may just have been the normal wanderlust of Americans and the hope for better things in a new state.

By the time of the move, Bill Whisenhunt was twelve years old. Like many rural people of that period, his family did not emphasize education. When asked, Whisenhunt said that he really did not know how long he went to school. He and his brothers and sisters would go to school for a few weeks in the winter and sometimes in other parts of the year when there were no chores or other work for them to do. He estimated that he probably had about the equivalent of an eighth-grade education, but that was just a guess.

Whisenhunt had a talent that few other people had and that continually amazed his children. Someone could call out a list of numbers, no matter how many or how large they might be, and when the person had finished calling out the numbers, Whisenhunt would immediately say what the total was. He never failed in this. He explained that when he went to school, he did not have a slate and chalk like most children on which to do his arithmetic, so he taught himself how to add numbers in his head as he heard them called out. He could not explain the technique or teach his children to do it.

Whisenhunt never gained any particular skills and usually worked as a farm laborer and in other manual labor jobs that were available. He did, however, become interested in games of chance and spent much time in pool rooms in the towns of Oklahoma, becoming quite a skilled pool player.

Whether Whisenhunt and Names were influenced directly by the Progressive movement under way during their youth is not known. Like Kansas, where Names grew up, the area of Texas where Whisenhunt spent his early years had been a hotbed of Populism in the 1890s. Whisenhunt was too young to remember the active days of Populism, but the ideology of the movement did not go away just because the political party faded from existence. Some of Whisenhunt's class-consciousness and concern about the "common people" clearly originated with his childhood environment. Given their later interests in public affairs, Names and Whisenhunt both were most likely influenced by the ideas and actions of men like Theodore Roosevelt and Woodrow Wilson.

When the United States entered World War I, Whisenhunt and his brother Noah Lewis enlisted in the army. Both were sent to France, but they never saw one another during their service. Bill never saw combat, but his brother was killed in action. Bill Whisenhunt did suffer an injury, however, when an automobile struck him on the street. His broken arm was not set properly and did not heal as it should have. Since he was in a war zone, the injury was officially war-related, and he had a partial disability for the rest of his life. He was not handicapped severely by this injury, but he did receive some benefits later on.

When he returned from the war, Whisenhunt could find little to do back in Oklahoma. He was at loose ends and did a few odd jobs from time to time, but before long, a friend suggested that they go to California to pursue their dreams. California had an attraction from the middle of the nineteenth century, and it still had a pull for young men of the Middle West and Plains States who thought they could find their fortune there. Whisenhunt agreed, and the two men set off. Since they had little money, they "rode the rails"—rode illegally on freight trains. They probably could not have been called "hoboes" in a technical sense, since they were not on the road permanently, but they lived the life of a hobo as much as any of the hoboes did.

In California they were disappointed as so many pilgrims to that state have been through the years. They were not able to find work and found themselves living in hobo "jungles" in southern California, where Whisenhunt's ideology and class-consciousness were strengthened. He often told the story of meeting a man in one of the jungles who was in his eighties and proudly proclaimed that he had never worked in his life to make other men rich. This man said that laborers were tolerated only because their labor made the rich richer and he refused to be a part of that system. So he lived by begging and scrounging what he could from garbage cans and other places. Whisenhunt never adopted the man's ideology, but it did make an impression on him. Except for the short periods during the Great Depression when he was on government relief, he was usually self-employed in some way.

After a period in California, Whisenhunt and his friend decided they should go home. They had not found their place in the world and were tired, hungry, homesick, and out of money. They hopped a freight and started home. Whisenhunt later told about how hungry they were and how he broke the law for the only time in his life. They were not too far from home, but they were so hungry that they were not sure they could make it. The two men went into a country store, and Whisenhunt convinced the shopkeeper to take a check from him. The check was for only about a dollar, but it is remarkable that the man accepted it from a total stranger. They bought some cheese and crackers with the money and then got back on the train. Whisenhunt said he really felt guilty about writing a bad check, and as soon as he got home, he borrowed money from his mother and deposited the money in the bank to cover the check.

When he returned to Oklahoma, Whisenhunt still did not find much to do and had no permanent way of making a living. He did odd jobs and farm work, but most of his work was temporary; he never seemed to have any interest in farming, the occupation of most of the people in his community. He played pool and dominoes and may have won some money from gambling. He was single and lived at home, so he did not have a lot of expenses.

In 1922 Whisenhunt and some friends decided to go to Texas to see if they could find work. By this time, the farm depression following World War I had set in and farmers were struggling just to stay alive. The young men thought they might be able to find work in the cotton harvest by "pulling bolls," hand-harvesting ripe cotton bolls. On this trip Whisenhunt met the woman who soon became his wife.

Beulah Johnson was born in Bokoshe, Oklahoma, on June 20, 1904, the daughter of Christopher Columbus and Nellie Green Johnson. She was one of the oldest of nine children. Her life had been as hard as if not harder than Whisenhunt's. Her father was a sharecropper in far eastern Oklahoma, one of the poorest areas of the territory at the time of her birth. He worked his children very hard, and several of the children had long-held resentments of the father. Beulah and her siblings were allowed to go to school only when there was nothing else to do, and she later estimated that she had the equivalent of a third-grade education. She was literate and prided herself in later life on the number of times she had read the Bible, but she was always self-conscious about her lack of education and probably allowed that insecurity to prevent her from doing things that she would have been quite capable of doing.

Sometime in the early 1920s the Johnson family had migrated to Texas in search of opportunity. Farmers were suffering everywhere, and her father, like so many other Americans in all periods, believed he could do better somewhere else. The family moved to the town of Munday in North-central Texas, fairly close to the Red River and the state of Oklahoma, two hundred miles or more west along the Red River from Fannin County where Whisenhunt was born.

When Whisenhunt and his friends came to Munday, they went to work in the cotton fields for Beulah Johnson's father. Whisenhunt later said that he knew the first time he saw Beulah that she was the woman for him. Their courtship was short and not very romantic, but that was fairly common in the rural areas of America at that time. During 1922 they drove to the town of Benjamin, the county seat of Knox County where Munday was located, and were married by a justice of the peace at the county courthouse.

Not long after they were married they returned to Erin Springs, Oklahoma, where Whisenhunt tried several different jobs. At one point, he had a trapline to trap animals for their fur, and he spent time with his brother George, who had a small country store in the town of Erin Springs. In 1923 Bill and Beulah had their first child, William Alexander Whisenhunt, Jr., known throughout his life as Junior. A second son, Kenneth, was born in 1927, and a third son, Oscar Lewis, came in 1928.

In 1929 the Whisenhunt family left Oklahoma and migrated to the West Texas town of Meadow. Beulah Whisenhunt said in later life that she did not care where they moved because she was afraid that her husband might get into trouble if he stayed in Oklahoma. She thought the actions of some of his associates were questionable, and she wanted to be away from them. The Whisenhunts apparently chose the town of Meadow because one of Bill's sisters, Linnie Pearl, and her husband were sharecropping on land not far from Meadow. The family stayed in Meadow for about a year and then returned to Oklahoma, but this was not a satisfactory arrangement, and the family moved back to Meadow, where they stayed the rest of Bill's life.

In Meadow, Whisenhunt tried several different ways of making a living, especially operating a gasoline station on some occasions. The first gas station on the main highway that ran through Meadow had a small apartment in back where the family lived a hand-to-mouth existence. At that time, it was relatively inexpensive to get started in a gas station since oil companies would extend credit to someone renting the business, with little investment needed. Whisenhunt operated the station without any help except that of his wife, who would fill in when he needed to go somewhere or had something else to do.

When the Great Depression reached its depth, Whisenhunt could not hold on. Fewer people were driving their cars, if they still had cars, and many expected gasoline to be sold on credit, which a small operator like Whisenhunt could not do. Eventually, he was forced out of the gas station and found himself, like so many other people in the 1930s, without work or any special skills. He worked at whatever odd jobs he could find. Fortunately for him and millions like him, the New Deal of Franklin D. Roosevelt offered some hope. Roosevelt's various relief measures made work available for millions who had not worked—at least steadily—for years. Whisenhunt and his wife were not too proud to take surplus commodities when they were offered, and he readily took jobs with the Works Progress Administration (WPA) and other New Deal programs to put food on the table and clothing on the backs of his family.

By the end of the decade, the economy was slowly improving and prospects looked a bit better. At the end of the Depression decade, in 1938, a fourth son, Donald Wayne, was born to the Whisenhunt family.

Not long after their fourth son was born, Whisenhunt had the opportunity to go back into business for himself. As with the gas station, he could open a pool hall with very little investment or up-front cash, and he thought the time was ripe for a pool hall in Meadow. Meadow was a village of only about five hundred people in the late 1930s, but it was a trade center for the surrounding area since the practice of shopping in larger towns ten, twenty, or thirty miles away had not yet become a common practice. The community was usually hungry for entertainment. The most common and reliable entertainment at the time was the radio, but it was still an expensive appliance that not everyone could afford. Whisenhunt believed there were enough men who had some disposable income to make it possible for his pool hall to succeed. The business did not make him a rich man, but it provided more than the New Deal relief programs did.

Whisenhunt had grown up around pool halls in Oklahoma and felt at home in them. In Texas the law was vague as to the legality of such businesses.

Some people thought they were bad influences on the community, a common attitude throughout the country for many years, and were dens of drinking and gambling. Indeed, some believed that pool was merely a vehicle for gambling and should be illegal. Billiards was much like horse racing in Texas; the law did not prohibit horse races, but gambling on them was illegal. Why run horse races, some asked, if one could not wager on them? Many people looked at pool the same way. Even if pool halls were not illegal, certain elements in a community wanted them kept out because of the detrimental impact they might have on the community, especially young boys.

Whisenhunt had an arrangement with county officials, apparently without any payoff, where they agreed not to interfere with his operation if there were no complaints about it. Thus, he was scrupulous about not allowing anyone in the building who was under seventeen years old, and he never allowed any gambling or drinking to take place on the premises. Meadow was a dry town, so any violation of the drinking laws would have been a reason for immediate closure. In effect, Whisenhunt made every effort to see that his business was not a public nuisance because he did not want to give any church or moralistic citizens reason to complain.

Possibly as early as the 1920s, Whisenhunt became acquainted with Art Names when he extended his circuit deeper into Texas. He came to Meadow when times were still relatively prosperous. Since Names usually erected his tent on a vacant lot not far from Whisenhunt's pool hall, it was logical that they should get to know one another. Names had little to do during the day besides routine maintenance on his rig, and Whisenhunt had little to do as well. He operated his pool hall alone and kept it open about sixteen hours a day. Mostly he monitored the games of pool, racked the balls, and collected his money when a game was over. He also had domino tables that required only that he monitor the progress of the games and collect his fee at the end of each one.

Names and Whisenhunt spent much time together and found they had compatible political views and other interests. Whisenhunt learned much about show business and the earlier successes of the Names shows. The Names show did not stay long in Meadow, as it did not in any town, but the show did come by more than once in a season.

When the Whisenhunt children were old enough, they joined other boys in meeting Art Names's show when it hit town and doing their part to erect the tent and set up the stage and the seats inside. Names gave free passes to the boys who helped him set up. The Whisenhunt boys were especially proud when they could approach the box office and present their passes to the ticket taker; they felt as if they had accomplished something.

By late 1938 and early 1939 the war clouds in Europe were becoming darker. With the aggressive actions of Hitler and Mussolini, many people were convinced that there would be another war. For Americans caught up in the pacifism of the 1930s, the major objective was to keep America out of the war; even before war began in 1939, American factories began to increase production to sell to Europe.

When Hitler invaded Poland in 1939, and Britain and France kept their treaty obligations to Poland by declaring war on Germany, World War II began. Immediately, American products, both manufacturing and agricultural, were in demand. Gradually prosperity began to return, even though it was slow in the farm belt where farmers had been depressed since the end of World War I.

Whisenhunt began his pool hall at the right time, and things went pretty well for him, enough so that he was able to accumulate modest savings. Suspicious of banks, especially since the massive failures at the beginning of the 1930s, Whisenhunt put his money in places only he knew about since he was not willing at this point to trust banks with his hard-earned money.

While things were beginning to go better for Whisenhunt, Names found his personal situation deteriorating. He and his wife divorced in 1939, and she soon remarried. He had no company and no money; all he had was his tent and other equipment and a worn-out truck that could usually be coaxed from one town to the next. Despite his destitution, Names resolved to continue with his show. He was not willing to give it up and work in some "normal" job.

During this period, Names traveled from town to town in areas where he was known. By this time, he had unofficially adopted Meadow, Texas, as his base of operations, coming to Meadow to spend the worst of the winter.

Names and Whisenhunt became better friends during this period. That friendship eventually blossomed into a business partnership.

FOUR

Feast or Famine

ART NAMES WAS FASCINATED—ONE MIGHT SAY OBSESSED—WITH show business from his childhood. While he was involved in many different activities, show business was always his life. He began to write plays early, probably by 1911, but it is likely he wrote dramatic readings and stage plays in his teenage years, if not earlier. His studious nature, as described by people who knew him when he was young, might have caused some to predict that he would be a scholar; but, in fact, he was more interested in people and wanted to do something to interact with others—and, above all, to entertain them.

He began early to perform his own works as well as plays written by others. Growing up in the time when vaudeville was still popular and towns had opera houses to accommodate the syndicates that sent out performers on a circuit, Names took advantage of the facilities available to stage his own productions. Living in a rural area with few professional performers, he often had local teenagers play the various parts.

Since the players were young amateurs, Names probably did not give them much freedom to interpret the parts, but he must have been a gentle director. Everyone who remembered him in the days before 1920—and after as well—commented on what a pleasant person he was. He seemed to have the ability to get along with almost everyone and to avoid conflict and confrontation. One high-school-age girl, Mayme Jones, who performed for him in communities around McCracken stated, "If he had not been well thought of I could not have run around the country like I did."[1]

Admission prices for his plays performed in opera houses or high school auditoriums are not known, except in a few instances. Whether he paid his actors is not known either. Mayme Jones said that his group of high school students played small towns around McCracken for several months. Most likely he paid them something, at least living expenses when they were on the road. Jones said that traveling began to tell on her grades, and her parents restricted her to performing only on weekends.[2]

In the period after World War I several touring tent shows played in various parts of Kansas. Names worked for some of them on occasion, but he clearly wanted to have his own operation and be in control. He and his cousin Leonard Ryan did rent or lease the McCracken opera house and other theaters from time to time to present plays.

Names was a restless soul. His wife said that he often wanted to do a one-man show, probably in the manner of Hal Holbrook doing Mark Twain many years later. She seemed to have reservations about his ability to do it, but as he never tried it, his potential for success was unproven. The thing he was most interested in during the early 1920s was taking his show into a tent. After about 1926 or 1927, he and Maurine began to look seriously for a tent, searching *Billboard* and reading classified ads in major city newspapers in the region. They finally found a large one in reasonable condition that had been used as a skating rink. Even used, it was still expensive. Art and Maurine were able to swing it financially, and they became a traveling company.

After they bought the tent, they needed something to live in on the road. Names found a medicine show wagon in Ulysses, Kansas, and bought it. He brought it to the fairgrounds, proudly showing it to his wife. "He took me out there and showed it to me, and I nearly flipped. I just nearly flipped," she remembered. "It was awful." It was a one-room trailer without a bathroom, fairly typical of house trailers or "house cars" as many people called them at the time. Maurine's father, who was visiting the show at the time, tried to make it more livable. He bought plywood, sealed it, and put in some light fixtures. Still, it was cramped and hot in the summer and cold in the winter.[3]

When the show went into a tent, Names tried to establish a routine, though it was difficult. He was imaginative, practical, and creative in his bookings, and he adapted to changing conditions. The company would play a town for a week at a time and present six or seven different plays—usually six, since Sundays were not performance nights except in rare instances. Many variations on the traveling routine were tried, such as three-night stands, where the show could play two towns per week. Another variation was the "circle stop": in the winter when it was too cold for the tent, the company would go back into theaters. Names would line up six towns and do one play per week, performing it six times, once in each town. The circle stop was not used very long after the company moved to the tent since it was not practical.

The tent season usually began in March or April, but that was subject to change. In fact, Names later tried to keep the tent operating year-round, and even though he could keep the tent warm, many people were skeptical of coming to a tent with piles of snow on the ground outside.[4] A clipping in the Names papers from a publication identified only as the *Hydro Review* was so complimentary of Art Names Company that it almost seems like a "puff piece" done by a newspaper at the behest of Names. The company was apparently appearing in a tent in the winter, as the publication said, "The tent is well heated and no one need fear being uncomfortable on account of the cold."[5]

Despite his success, Names was concerned about how he might be accepted outside the region where he was known. His wife said he would not go out of Kansas for quite a number of years, but he eventually ventured to cross the state line into Oklahoma and then into Texas. He found a favorable reception in both of those states, and they became regular territories for him. As he ventured farther from home, he stayed out longer in the season, especially where cotton was grown. He tried to stay long enough in the autumn to play to the migrant workers who came through to harvest the cotton.

Despite his hesitancy to leave the state, Maurine indicated that Names wanted to take his show to New York. The legitimate stage in New York was like Mecca to most theatrical people, and to play New York would be the pinnacle of success. On two or three different occasions he planned to go to New York, and once, at least, he worked about eighteen months with the same cast preparing to make the move. Despite his goal, he was never able to take the show to New York.[6]

By about 1929 Names had enough money to achieve his dream of replacing the skating rink tent he'd been using for several years with a new tent built to his specifications. Besides buying a new tent and sets for the stage, he and Maurine bought five new Ford trucks and a semi-trailer on which he had the stage built so that it could be moved more easily. Art Names Shows now had $55,000 worth of equipment sitting on the lot, an enormous investment at the time.[7]

During the same period a strain could be seen in the marriage. To have three children within three years, as Art and Maurine did, was a bit overwhelming to Maurine, who was still very young herself and had no experience with children. Art had no experience either. Learning to cope with babies probably was not much of an obstacle for a normal family, but the Names family was far from normal, changing towns—or "homes"—every three days or each week.[8]

Caring for the children proved to be a challenge. Finding someone in each town to do the laundry for the babies was difficult.[9] Jean, one of the twins, was a sickly child who was small and weak and often would not eat. Doctors told Maurine that he was going to die if something was not done to get him to eat. Art and Maurine were advised that goat milk would be good for him, so they bought a pedigreed goat for $75, an enormous sum at the time. When the show moved, the goat went on top of the equipment on the back of the truck. The goat proved to be a finicky eater—another trial for a family on the road.[10] Gradually, Jean grew stronger, and the danger to his health was not as serious.

When the trials of raising the three children became more than Maurine could handle, she and Art left the twins, and possibly Art, Jr., on occasion, to be cared for by a family named Derthick in the panhandle of Oklahoma.[11] Mr. and Mrs. Bryon Derthick, show-business midgets for a time, were acquainted with the Names family and agreed to take the boys into their home when they were very young. The Derthicks had a daughter of their own, Hazel, who was only a few years older. During the years the boys were with her family, she grew to think of Jack and Jean as her brothers.[12]

Caring for the children was difficult for the Derthicks, especially during the Depression years. Apparently, Art and Maurine were not always prompt in sending money, and they were hard to find at times. Hazel Derthick said that they sometimes had to track Art and Maurine down by person-to-person phone calls in towns from Kansas, Oklahoma, and Texas. How long the children stayed with the Derthicks is not clear. Hazel Derthick says they lived with her family from 1925 to 1937, but that is hard to document.[13] Since the twins were not born until 1927, this would mean that Art, Jr., was also placed with the Derthicks—which may, in fact, be true. Jack said that he and his brother were placed with the family when they were sixteen months old, and they did not go back to the show until they were close to eight years old, which would be 1935.[14]

Jack explained some of the confusion he and Jean experienced. He said that Mama and Papa "Derthy" called themselves governor and governess, but in truth they were more like parents. Jack said he and Jean were often confused about their parents and "wondered who our parents were—whether it was Mama Gerty and Daddy Byron or whether it was Daddy Art and Mother Maurine." Jack remembered, "Mother Maurine was always painted as a very beautiful, glorious magnificent actress, wonderful woman, you know, and I don't know—it was kind of hard to decide who our parents really were. We used to have talks about this wondering."[15] In the Names papers are two letters addressed to "Daddy Art" written on lined elementary school paper by the twins in the first two or three grades of school while they were with the Derthicks. These two letters were preserved by Art Names until his death and were kept in his papers afterward.[16]

When Maurine and Art were divorced in 1939, the twins were only twelve years old. Records indicate that the children remained with the Derthicks after they went to California, even though Hazel wrote that her family went to California in 1937 and that the twins lived with them only until 1935.[17] Hazel Derthick said that she and her parents appeared as Munchkins in the motion picture, *The Wizard of Oz*.[18] This may have been the reason they went to California, or they may have auditioned for the parts after they were there.

Byron Derthick wrote a letter to Art after they went to California, which would have been in 1939 or after. His family was almost destitute, living on Hazel's wages from the WPA. In the letter he complains about his "boarders," meaning Maurine and her new boyfriend or husband, a man identified as Slim Worthington. In fact, he asks Art if they are indeed married, since they sleep together. He complains that Maurine and her friend's coming to them was "one of the worst impositions I ever heard of." He says the unwelcome guests were "broke flat" and had to hock their car in Tucson, Arizona, to get money to get to California. They use his car and the small amount of gasoline he has running down worthless advertisements for jobs. To make matters worse, he says, the twins "are more impudent and disobedient since she came than before and I can see the hand writing on the wall unless some miricle [*sic*] takes place." Derthick says he is not a complainer but that he thought Art should know what was going on since the boys are his and he should be concerned about them. Art, Jr., must have been with Art at the time since Derthick closes his letter, "Best wishes to you and Snookie," a nickname for Art, Jr., when he was very young.[19]

Even when the twins were in their teenage years, the issue of guardianship was still a matter of concern. In 1944, when they were seventeen, they were placed in the custody of a Mr. Roy Thurston of Afton, Texas, who may have been a school official in that town. An undated and unsigned letter in the Names papers states that Jack and Jean are under the "full control and legal guardianship of Mr. Roy Thurston of Afton, Texas, in locis [*sic*] parentis." The letter says that this action has the approval of Art, his ex-wife, and her new husband, the stepfather of the twins. Thurston was to have "complete con- trol ... until the boys have finished their high school education and have been inducted into the army." The letter concludes with a statement from Art that this action is necessary because his "business keeps me constantly on the move, which condition was plainly not for the best interest of the boys involved."[20] On April 15, 1944, Names received a telegram while he was in Ropes, Texas, from Thurston saying there was some "protest concerning guardianship of boys" and asking him to "prepare sworn statement and send as soon as possible."[21] Since the letter is undated, it may have been the telegram that prompted the letter mentioned above.

Clearly, the Names family situation was not typical of normal families during the 1920s and 1930s. Show business has always had its special strains on families. People who knew the Nameses almost always reported how Art doted on Maurine, possibly because she was so young when they married. She had been raised in a show-business environment and may not have known very much about coping with the real world. Some said she was very demanding and could be petulant if she did not get her way. Her inability to cope with her children adequately may have been a reflection of her immaturity. Art, for whatever reason, did seem to be dominated by Maurine.

Though the Names tent show prospered during the 1920s, by the 1930s, farmers could not afford the few pennies that Names charged. From his pinnacle in 1929 with the purchase of new equipment, Names's show began to decline.

Names's business success can be evaluated to some extent since his federal income tax returns for 1926 to 1939 have survived. The return for 1930 is unreadable, and in 1931 and 1935 the business receipts and expenses are unreadable. Even so, an analysis of this fourteen-year period reveals the ups and downs of the Names operation. Since federal income taxes did not exist before the passage of the Nineteenth Amendment to the Constitution in 1913, the paying of personal income taxes was still a relatively new experience. During these years, no one paid taxes on an adjusted income of $4,000 or less, an amount that exempted a major portion of the population. Adjusted income was calculated by deducting a personal exemption and dependent exemptions from total income. During only one of these years, 1926, did Names pay any income taxes, and that was $35.53 on a total income of $6,543.41.[22] On one occasion, Names completed his tax returns and told his wife that it was not as bad as it looked. She remembered, "He said actually we cleared more money than John D. Rockefeller did." That was because the tax laws were such that millionaires like Rockefeller had tax lawyers who could use the loopholes to show that someone like him did not make any profit during a given year. Maurine said they were grateful for what they made and knew they were better off than others. She mentioned a banker friend of theirs in McCracken who "had gone to the wall . . . and one night in the bank shot himself." She said she believed they had cleared more than $10,000 that year.[23] Evidently she was mistaken; the records show that they never made that much between 1926 and 1939.

The profit from his show business was his only income, and despite increasing hard times, he had a profit every year from 1926 to 1939. Names apparently did not pay himself or his wife a regular salary, and their living expenses came from the profits. If he had paid salaries to the two of them, undoubtedly the show would have showed a loss in some years. Show-business profit ranged from a high of $7,909.48 in 1929 to a low of $1,723.50 in 1932. From 1926 to 1931 total profit was more than $3,000 per year, but it could and did change drastically from year to year, as when their profit dropped from $6,543.41 in 1926 to $3,040.49 the next year. Why there would be such a change in one year is not clear. On the 1926 return Names showed a loss from a fire that included his tent at $950 and chairs at $150. In 1927 he did not show any unusual expenses, but he may have charged the cost of tent replacement to 1927 and thus reduced his income. There is just enough information in these tax returns to raise many other questions. For example, during the 1920s he listed a significant deduction for depreciation of equipment. It was always more than $2,000 per year, but in 1929 he claimed a deduction of $3,289, a reflection, probably, of all the new equipment he purchased that year.

Another discrepancy in the tax records needs clarification. The year of Names's lowest personal profit was 1939, when he reported only $1,551.71 in income. This is misleading, however, since he had a partner that year and the profit was double the amount, $3,103.43, which they split equally. The figures from 1939 are puzzling for another reason. By 1939 most historians agree that the Depression was abating and that, in fact, prosperity was returning with the outbreak of war in Europe in September and the increasing demands for American products that President Roosevelt had been providing to the Allies for more than a year. Yet Names's operation did not show much improvement in 1939 over the other years of the 1930s.

Perhaps the best way to analyze the show's success is to compare the year-by-year receipts and expenses. During this fourteen-year period, the show's largest receipts were in the first year, 1926, when Names reported $27,967.36, but his most profitable year was 1929 when receipts were $26,606.33. Clearly, as receipts declined during the 1930s, Names did all he could to reduce expenses. After 1920, when his income dropped drastically, he stopped listing depreciation as a deductible expense. That might be explained by the fact that he did not need that expense to avoid paying taxes, but, more likely, it reflected the declining value of his equipment.[24] When his wife was asked if they had to sell the trucks when hard times came, she said, "We didn't sell all of anything. They finally just disintegrated. I don't know what became of the trucks."[25] A woman from Kansas, Marian Winter, said the Names show was one of the few bright spots during the long, hot summers of the Depression. She hinted that Names was liked by the country people because he was as down on his luck as they were. She said that in 1934 and 1935 times were hard for everyone, and Names's "tent had so many patches it looked like a crazy quilt." Names seemed to have inspired confidence as Winter said that the summer storms on the plains would blow up with high winds and lightning flashing, but the old tent somehow held together. She said, "If Art told us to just set [sic] tight, that *he* was watching the storm, we believed him & sat happily chewing the candy that they sold between acts."[26]

The extent of his lack of success can be seen in the receipts in 1926 of almost $28,000 dropping to a low of $5,860 in 1938. There is a corresponding decline in expenses, as well, but it is clear that Art Names Shows was barely surviving by the end of the 1930s.[27]

Names seems to have been a person concerned about doing the right thing regarding his taxes. For example, in 1937 he wrote a letter from a town in Oklahoma to the Treasury Department concerning the payment of social security taxes, a new law in its first year of operation. Names asked several questions about the collection and payment of social security taxes, but in the course of the letter he revealed some of his personality and the hard times he was going through. He called himself "one of Uncle Sam's Delinquent nephews" who was sending overdue taxes. "Would have sent August in before but I was too hard up. Business has been very bad and I cut my show down to one man and my wife and I—that's all I'm using except a little manual labor to put the tent up and take it down." He said he had been sick for two weeks but the local banker "saw me thru or my dear Uncle would have lost a taxpayer, but I think I am getting on my feet now but my finances are still none too good."[28]

The point of his letter was to ask if he should collect social security taxes from the boys and sometimes men that he hired in each town to help him put up and take down the tent—sometimes only for an hour or two. He was not sure if he should list all these people as employees, particularly since most of them were farm boys who were not eligible to participate in social security and did not have social security numbers. Interestingly, this whole matter could not have involved more than a few cents in each town, but Names was careful to try to do the right thing, even if he was delinquent.

People who remembered Names sometimes thought he had to leave show business during the Depression years. Most of these were people who did not know him well and whose memories many years later were not very reliable. One of those men was Rolland Haverstock, another tent show operator, who said Names was closed in the 1930s and reopened about 1940 or 1944.[29] A woman in Kansas believed that he "broke up his show while in Zenda one late summer night. He didn't have enough cash to pay his actors to get home."[30] Maurine Names remembered that during the worst of the Depression, they stored the tent and she and Art went back into theaters. By this point they were down to just the two of them. She could not remember the years when they did this, and it is difficult to piece together specifically when it might have been. A woman who had worked on the show wrote that she joined the Art Names operation in 1933 when she married one of the actors. They stayed with Names until 1937. If her memory is accurate, the tent was used during those years.[31] An analysis of the expenses claimed on Names's income tax returns suggests that he may have closed the tent for only one year.

During these hard years, Names, like most other entertainment entrepreneurs, did what he could to stimulate business. He had nights when women were admitted free and sometimes conducted contests, such as "pretty girl" contests in which the contestants were men dressed as women. He gave free admission on occasion, hoping that his sales of candy and popcorn to a full house would be equal to or better than the admission receipts.[32] He even made arrangements for the publication of comic books with a company that specialized in various promotions. It had a generic masked hero named Spirit who was little more than a copy of Superman or Captain Marvel. The company printed at the top of the cover, "Art Names Comic Weekly. A Publication of Art Names & Sons Your Favorite Entertainers," a common practice then and now in which companies can customize publications for their customers at minimal cost. Judging from the wording of the title, this may have been published after 1939, when Names and his wife were divorced. There is no evidence that Names continued this arrangement, probably because of the cost and the questionable value it may have had. Only one issue has survived.[33]

Hard times took its toll on the Names family. Whatever specific problems existed between Art and Maurine have not been discussed by anyone who would know the details, but by 1939 the differences became pronounced enough that they were divorced. The following year the wife of his former partner, Joe Sims, wrote Art: "Which is hardest? You lost your love to the 'living.' I lost mine to 'Death.' Death is so 'final' while there is 'life there is hope.' She may come back someday."[34] This reference suggests that Maurine left Art for another man; she did remarry fairly quickly to Slim Worthington, a friend of both of them who may have been an actor on the show.

Art continued the show without his wife. During 1939 he had a partner, Jack Campbell, and in early 1940 he indicated in a letter to a film company that he had five people on his show. This may still have been during the Campbell partnership, but he was asking about buying a 16mm motion picture projector since he wanted to mix live shows with film.[35] He may have been looking toward only showing motion pictures.

Art Names had suffered numerous blows. He was almost out of business by 1940, and his marriage had broken up. Even though the nation's economy was recovering from the depression, his future looked bleak. During low spots such as these, a person's character is tested; in Names's case he was not found wanting. Art Names was a man of resilient character. A weaker person would have been overwhelmed by the problems he faced after his divorce in 1939. With his tent show's fortunes going up and down during late 1939 and early 1940, the average person probably would have folded the operation and tried to find work in the recovering economy, especially the factories now supplying the Allied powers in their desperate struggle against fascism in Europe. But Names was not a typical person. By 1940 he was almost fifty years old, and he had always done things his own way. If there was any way he could keep his show operating, he was going to do it.

The existing records are not complete about this stage of Names's life, but a reasonably accurate picture can be assembled from sketchy records. After his divorce in 1939, Maurine left the show. Art, Jr., stayed with his father some of the time, and the twins apparently were in California with the Derthicks.[36] The relationship between Art and Maurine remained friendly, with Art helping out occasionally, as he did in early 1940 when he sent her some money because he thought she was about to "go on the rocks."[37] Some people believed that Maurine went to California to try to get into motion pictures. By 1940 Milburn Stone had established himself in Hollywood as a minor character actor; Maurine thought that she was as good an actor as Stone and that perhaps this was her opportunity.[38]

Maurine and Slim Worthington were eventually married, but Art continued to try to help his former wife and they corresponded on a regular basis. One of the few surviving letters from her to Art is undated, but it appears to have been written in 1940. It is a friendly letter addressed to "Dear Pappy" or "Dear Poppy." She says she received a letter from the twins saying they needed money. She talks about clothes she bought for them and a hat she bought for herself. The letter is damaged, but she seems to indicate that she has remarried.[39]

Maurine apparently had a difficult time after the divorce. She and Slim stayed for a while with the Derthicks in California, as mentioned earlier.[40] On another occasion, Art wrote her a lengthy letter giving advice and trying to help her find a way to make some money. On one occasion, he suggested to Maurine that she could try to make some money by rewriting one of his plays, *Are You a Monkey?*, in a simpler version and producing it in high school auditoriums with high school actors. He gave her a great deal of specific advice.[41] Whether she ever presented the play is not known.

Names had concerns about his children who were living with other people, his former wife who seemed to be floundering, and his own business. During 1939 Names was in partnership with Jack Campbell, but when this arrangement ended is not clear. His letter in January, 1940, to a film company suggests that the partnership with Campbell was continuing.[42] In another letter at about the same time, he wrote to a friend that "only having one woman on the show limits greatly the plays we can use." Presumably, this one woman was Jack Campbell's wife.[43] Within a month, Names was writing to friends about how his show was down to Art, Jr., and himself.[44] Names was still with Campbell in late 1939 or early 1940. In the Names papers are two undated advertising brochures that refer to Names as the "Foremost 1940 Candidate for Governor of Kansas," and both brochures advertise two of Names's antiwar plays, *We, Who Are Fools!* and *The Fighting Fool!* that feature Jack and Ilaferne Campbell.[45] Names's candidacy was at least partly an attempt to get publicity as a means of improving his business. Yet he convinced some people that he was a candidate, a fact they remembered twenty years later.[46]

The Names-Campbell partnership ended early in 1940, and Names was down to showing motion pictures by himself or with his son when he was with him. Without doubt, 1940 was the low point for Names. A lesser man would have given up—but not Names. He struggled to keep his show open but was never sure from day to day that he would be able to do so. W. H. Fluitt from Booker, Texas, in the far northern panhandle, wrote that Names and his son showed movies in Booker. "Of course, he didn't have very good movies, but what the hell, it was still Art Names & people went anyway." When Names discovered that Fluitt had just bought two new tires for his truck, he talked to him about buying the old tires since used tires were probably better than the ones he had. Fluitt gave Art the tires. He remembered, "Art hadn't lost his pride though, he gave me some passes to the show in exchange."[47] In the early months of 1940 Names wrote to friends several times about how hard things were. In February he wrote from Anton, Texas, about twenty miles northwest of Lubbock, and said he had done a little better that week, but not much. The night before, he and his son put on a "concert"—he did not indicate just what that consisted of—that brought in receipts of $4.15.[48] That he could continue with such small receipts is startling.

In March he wrote to Helen B. Ross Sims that he had made a "long jump and like to never made it" from Lorenzo, Texas, near Lubbock to Lipscomb, Texas, in the extreme northeast corner of the panhandle, at least 150 miles from Lorenzo. Considering the condition of his equipment, this was, indeed, a long move. He said when he got loaded up, his truck did not have the power to pull the house car and he had to leave it in Lorenzo with friends. He had to make the long jump without the trailer because weather was unpredictable and he might not have the money later. He planned to go back to get the trailer as soon he could since expenses for him and his son were much higher without the trailer to live in. He told his friend, "I am still riding the ragged edge of nothing—I marvel at how I am able to hang on to such a slender thread without snapping it—some day I suppose I will get my feet tangled up in something and take a real nose dive—" Despite his desperate situation, Names was always optimistic. He said, "With six bits in my pocket I am still dealing in million dollar ideas and am still going to make a terriffic [sic] impression on the world? Do you get as big a laugh out of that as I do?" Names was able to laugh at himself, a trait that no doubt contributed to his survival. "I don't think I am so funny when on the stage but in real life I feel that I am the world's greatest comedian—In my saddest and most serious moments I hand myself the most terriffic [sic] laughs."[49]

At his lowest moment, Names found a savior in the person of Bill Whisenhunt. This was not something that happened overnight. Names and Whisenhunt had known each other for several years as Names played the town of Meadow on a regular basis.

When Names came to Texas sometime in the 1920s, he found the small towns around Lubbock—towns like Afton, Anton, Lorenzo, New Home, Ropes (Ropesville), and Meadow—to be especially receptive to his kind of entertainment, welcoming him year after year, even when he was down on his luck and was showing the same movies again and again. Art called this his "good country." These little towns ranged in population from about two hundred to as many as a thousand, but they provided loyal audiences—and friends—that Names never forgot. He was extremely good with people in general, but he was especially good at remembering names, and that always impressed the country people who looked upon him as a personal friend.

In 1941, while the partnership with Whisenhunt was pending, Names decided to take advantage of his reputation in the neighboring town of Ropes (Ropesville), about six miles from Meadow. In April of that year the Ropes newspaper announced that Names was going to open a movie theater in the town. Names said, "Ropes is entitled to a good picture show, and I believe from now on through the summer a show on Friday night would be appreciated. People like good clean entertainment and a place where they can relax and enjoy themselves and there is no need for them to have to drive 20 or 30 miles to see a show when it can be produced at home for half the price." He clearly was playing on community pride and hoping his reputation would help the venture succeed. The editor knew Names and praised him, saying, "The proprietor of this new movie house will be none other than Art Names, who so many times in the past has brought his stage show into our midst, and knows personally almost every man, woman and child in our territory."[50] At this point in his life, Names was trying anything he could to survive the hard times. No records exist as to what happened to the Ropes movie theater, but it was during that summer that the Names-Whisenhunt partnership was formed. One would assume that the Ropes show did not survive the summer.

Names did what he could to ingratiate himself with individual communities. For example, in 1931 he joined the American Legion post in Muleshoe, Texas, a small town about seventy miles northwest of Lubbock, a town that always turned out for his show.[51] During his travels he always maintained his home base of McCracken, Kansas, and mail was forwarded to him from there to wherever he was about every two weeks. He decided to change his base of operations in 1940 to Meadow, Texas. In January he was still writing a film distributor that his permanent home base was McCracken, but a short time later he wrote the same company to say that his permanent address was Meadow, Texas.[52]

Meadow was one of his "good towns." An undated clipping from the *Meadow Star*, the local newspaper, gives a hint of his experiences there. The newspaper reviewed two new plays by Names and agreed that they were the two best plays he had presented there during the previous ten years,[53] a period when Names got to know Meadow well enough to begin to use it as his base of operations.

The member of the Whisenhunt family who was most taken with show business of the Names variety was the eldest son, Junior Whisenhunt. He was a high school student by the end of the 1930s and was enthralled by the scenes he saw on the stage. Junior seemed to have much potential. On one occasion when he was younger, he had entered, without his parents' knowledge, an essay contest run by the *Meadow Star* for essays on what could be done to make Meadow grow. When he won, his parents were very proud. The contest provided only a modest prize for winning, but as in any small community, the honor and community recognition were more important.

When Names was in Meadow, he and Whisenhunt had many conversations. In the early years before the Names divorce, Maurine often made coffee in their trailer house and Whisenhunt would visit for a cup of coffee and keep an eye on his business across the street.

Names talked about show business, and Whisenhunt was interested in hearing about it. Many times during the summer or after school in other times of the year, Junior Whisenhunt might join these conversations, enthralled by the stories of traveling with the show. Maurine Names liked Junior and talked to him about show business.

Whisenhunt's wife, who was quite religious, liked Art and Maurine, which was surprising, given the fact that show business was not always considered respectable, show people often being shunned in the communities where they played. Art was so personable and outgoing that he overcame the resistance of most people. Whisenhunt's wife got along with Maurine but was never very comfortable around her. Maurine was younger and was an attractive, flashy show-business type of person. Whisenhunt's wife thought their way of life was difficult and probably not good for children, but she did seem to think that Art and Maurine did a good job of raising their children. She may not have been aware that Art and Maurine placed the children as infants with the Derthicks.

After the divorce in 1939, Art continued to play Meadow, first with his Campbell partnership, then alone when he was showing movies. During those bad times for him, he would come to Meadow and set up his tent for the winter months. He owned only a few prints of motion pictures, mostly Westerns and one Tarzan feature film, and he showed them over and over during the winter. Although Meadow residents were loyal customers, even they had a limit to how many times they would watch the same film. Some nights no one came to the show.

During this time, the Whisenhunts often invited Names to their home for home-cooked meals; he was grateful for the friendship and felt close to them. During the many conversations between Whisenhunt and Names at the pool hall and at the Whisenhunt home, Names talked about his desire to get his stage show on the road again. He saw an opportunity with the recovering economy and bemoaned the fact that he was so destitute that he could not go on the road again. He said that if he could get the show operational again, he believed that he could get his former wife to return as the leading lady, and his three sons were old enough to be performers. Even his former wife's new husband was an actor of sorts and Names believed that he might also be available if the show got back on the road.[54]

No one knows who first broached the subject of Whisenhunt joining Names in this venture. Whatever the case, Whisenhunt made the decision around 1941 to invest in Art Names Shows, and Names accepted him as an equal partner. Whisenhunt had saved a bit of money after he opened the pool hall, and he invested about eight hundred dollars in the new venture. Even though they were equal partners, Names clearly was the one with the experience and the knowledge to make the show work—if, indeed, it could work.[55]

Another remarkable fact was that Whisenhunt's wife was willing for her husband to invest all they had in such a risky enterprise, especially one in which her husband had no experience. She had been so scarred by the hard times of the Depression that one would have expected her to insist on investments that offered more security, but she did agree to the venture. The convincing factor for her may well have been the enthusiasm of her eldest son, Junior Whisenhunt, who was so interested in show business.

Names had stored his stage equipment at various places, mostly in Kansas. He needed money to retrieve the equipment and refurbish it as best he could for the new show. Names knew the tent had deteriorated badly over the past several years and significant maintenance was needed just to get a respectable-looking tent operation back on the road.

He also had to dust off his scripts and in some instances rewrite them to accommodate the cast he would have. The new operation would have only one female actor, his former wife, if she were willing to return with the children. In some instances, he would not be able to rewrite all his scripts to have only one female character; in those cases, one of the male actors would have to play a female role. To make matters worse, the only adult actors on the new

FEAST OR FAMINE

show were Names and his former wife—and occasionally her new husband. The other actors were all teenage boys—the three sons of Names and Junior Whisenhunt. Whisenhunt had two other sons, Kenneth and Lewis, who were younger than Junior but who might possibly be available as actors sometime in the future. They were so young that for them to play older characters would have required significant makeup magic or the audience's good faith. Names could rewrite the scripts to some extent, but he could not completely write out characters who were older and still be creditable. Whisenhunt would not do any acting and, at first, did not travel on the show. He actually had no plans to do so because he was going to continue to run the pool hall for additional income, and only when law enforcement officials closed the pool hall did he go on the road. He said he would do manual labor, but he was not an actor.[56]

Maurine Names later said that she was dumbfounded when Art told her that he had entered a partnership with Whisenhunt. She said, "I was really just knocked for a loop when he first told me . . . I just couldn't imagine it, you know, because he never had before and always he turned down any suggestion of anybody for a partnership."[57] Actually, her memory was faulty since she did not recall the Sims and Campbell partnerships, but she was correct in that Names usually eschewed involvement with others where he might not have total control.

Members of the Names family were impressed with Whisenhunt. Maurine said that Art must have "recognized something in . . . [Whisenhunt] that he really admired and respected or he never would have . . . joined with him as a partner."[58] Jack Names remembered that Whisenhunt was "a really interesting, exciting character." He thought Whisenhunt was an excellent judge of people and that he was able to run a pool hall successfully because of "his knowledge of people's psyche, the gambling, the pool hall thing, his knowledge of people." He was "a nice guy, but a very sharp person when it came to dealing with people." He said there were many differences between Names and Whisenhunt, but there were many similarities as well. Whisenhunt "was a very fair person and I think that's why he and my dad respected each other because they were fair, they were honest, they knew people." He said Whisenhunt was "really a bright, interesting guy. Really kind of exciting to be around, good-natured; he and Dad, they kind of made a team. . . . And they were really good friends."[59] Maurine agreed: "But he said to me, Art himself said to me, 'I don't know at times where I would have been if it hadn't have been for Whisenhunt.'"[60]

Once the business deal was struck, Names was anxious to get started. He did not want to wait until his family could return to the show. He took Whisenhunt's investment, made minor repairs on the tent, and began to rent films that people had not seen before.

Junior Whisenhunt was probably the most excited about this new arrangement. As soon as the deal was made, Names agreed that Junior could go with him on the road to show films. Names was hoping to make some money while he was waiting for his family to return—an invitation that Maurine had accepted—and he could retrieve his stored equipment while on the road. Whisenhunt and his wife agreed that Junior could go with Names while Whisenhunt remained at home running his pool hall.

Names and Junior Whisenhunt left immediately, moving the tent to Plains, Texas, a small community about forty miles southwest of Meadow. They stayed there for two or three weeks, moving next to Benjamin, Texas, about 150 miles east of Meadow. Benjamin was another "good town," and they stayed there for several weeks. During that time, Beulah Whisenhunt went to Benjamin a few times to see Junior and to visit her parents who lived in Munday, Texas, only fifteen or so miles from Benjamin. There is a certain irony in this since Benjamin was the town where Bill and Beulah had gone from Munday in 1922 to get married.

The initial response to the new Art Names Show was encouraging. Old friends came out to see Names; business was good enough in Benjamin that they could stay there several weeks. Whisenhunt was doing well at home with the pool hall, and the future seemed to hold promise. The two younger Whisenhunt sons, Kenneth and Lewis, became excited about what their older brother was doing, and they began to agitate to go on the road as well. For the time being, that was not to be the case, but after Whisenhunt's business was closed and he joined the tent show on the road, the other two sons went with him.

At the time, things looked good for Names. He had had his dark days, but they seemed to be ending. He had no way of knowing that the Whisenhunt partnership would be his last significant foray into show business. The clock was ticking on his career and his life.

Maurine Allen Names in the 1920s,
probably about the time she married
Names. COURTESY OF THE NAMES FAMILY.

Art Names in uniform during
World War I.
COURTESY OF RUTH STUMP.

Art Names and his 7th and 8th grade
classes when he was a teacher in
McCracken, Kansas, in 1914.
COURTESY OF RUTH STUMP.

Milburn Stone, who got his professional start with Art Names in 1922, as the character he made famous, "Doc" Adams, on the long-running television show, Gunsmoke. COURTESY OF MILBURN STONE.

The "housecar" that Art Names bought for his bride and that he continued to use for the rest of his life. COURTESY OF THE NAMES FAMILY.

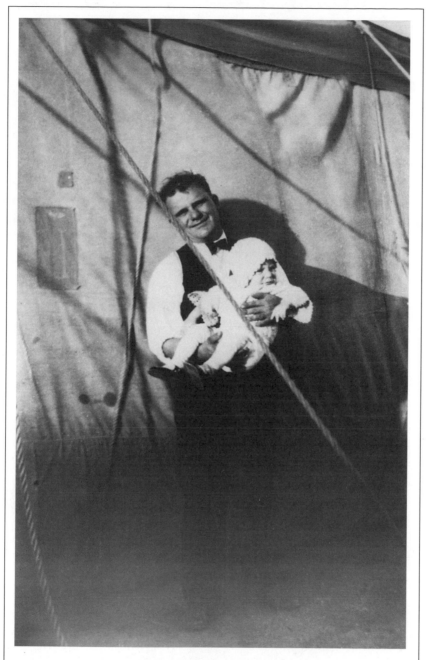

Art Names holding his first-born,
Art, Jr., outside the tent during the 1920s.
COURTESY OF THE NAMES FAMILY.

VOTE FOR NAMES!

Candidate for office

some time

in

the near future.(maybe.)

***

Politics will be clean
at
last.

***

WHoo- ray! W-H-O-O-P-E-E.

*This political flyer was probably created in the
1920s when Art Names was considering a career
in politics but had not yet decided when he
would run or what office he would seek.*

COURTESY OF CAROLYN THOMPSON.

No3

MAUHNE
&
ART

*One of the five trucks bought in the 1920s
when the show was at its most prosperous.*

COURTESY OF THE NAMES FAMILY.

The Names twins probably in Oklahoma with the daughter of the family that raised them when their parents decided they needed help with the children. LEFT TO RIGHT: *Jean Names, Hazel Derthick Resmondo, and Jack Names.* COURTESY OF THE NAMES FAMILY.

Arthur Names, ca. late 1930s.
COURTESY OF THE NAMES FAMILY.

*Art Names in costume and makeup as either the
G-String character or the Sputters character.*
COURTESY OF THE NAMES FAMILY.

*A highway accident that wreaked
havoc with Art Names Shows,
ca. late 1920s or early 1930s.*
COURTESY OF THE NAMES FAMILY.

Art Names emerging from his "housecar"
in Meadow, Texas. Note the town name on the water tower.

The tent for Art Names Shows in the 1930s.
Note the two patches on the top of the tent.

Box office of Art Names Show in the 1940s.

Storefront advertising for Art Names Shows during World War II.

Art Names and a local girl inside the tent somewhere in Kansas during the 1940s.

Scene from Deep in the Heart of Texas, *probably performed in Kansas in the 1940s.* LEFT TO RIGHT: *Art Names, Jr., "Slim" Worthington, and Maurine Names Worthington.*

Scene from Are You a Monkey? *during World War II.* LEFT TO RIGHT: *Art Names, Jr., probably Jack Names, and Maurine Names Worthington.*

Billboard advertising for Art Names Show,
ca. 1930s.

Art Names, Jr., (LEFT) and William "Junior" Whisenhunt in Meadow, Texas, while Whisenhunt was on furlough after basic training in World War II.

The Whisenhunt family after the partnership with Names ended. LEFT TO RIGHT:
Lewis, Kenneth, Beulah, and William "Bill." In front is Donald Wayne.

FIVE

On the Road Again

GETTING ART NAMES SHOWS BACK ON THE ROAD REQUIRED MORE than an infusion of money. The money was necessary, of course, but organizing a traveling stage show required much planning, extensive experience, and a great deal of luck. Art Names had the experience and was good at planning; his luck had not been very good in recent years, but now he was hoping that he was due for a change.

Immediately after the partnership was formed, Names took off with the tent to show motion pictures, taking Whisenhunt's oldest son with him. His purpose was to test the territory to see if people who remembered him would come back to his show, especially now that he had the money to rent films that the audiences had not seen before. His hope was to make some money, if possible, and to assist with the restoration of the stage show. Names told people in his old territory that he was going to bring the live show back to them, and most people reacted favorably.[1]

Names was taking a serious risk. Repertoire shows had been declining in popularity for several years, and a number of them had gone out of business. The most immediate cause, certainly, was the depression of the 1930s, but tent shows were facing other challenges. Motion pictures were becoming more popular each year, and 1939 was a landmark year with both *The Wizard of Oz* and *Gone With the Wind* being released. Movie theaters were more comfortable than in the past, especially as air conditioning and efficient heating systems were developed. Moreover, movies were cheap. Stage shows were not expensive, but they did have expenses that required a regular infusion of cash on a daily basis to stay on the road, while motion picture theaters could endure small crowds more than the stage shows could. The return of prosperity also brought more opportunities for people to be entertained in a variety of ways. This was possible now because automobiles were easier to obtain and entertainment in more distant locations was feasible.

Names was always an optimist, and now was no exception. With the Whisenhunt partnership, he believed that his hard times were over. As soon as the partnership was arranged, Names wrote to his former wife to see if she would return as the leading lady on his new show and bring the children to be actors as well. She was remarried by this time, but that was no impediment to a good relationship. Maurine was as optimistic as he was. She said, "I went back on the show and started building the show again just as friends; it was strictly platonic." She said it was a business deal. No records exist as to the financial arrangement he made with her, but apparently it was agreeable to all parties. She said of Art, "He couldn't get what he wanted without me and I was pretty lost out of show business without him. The two of us together made a darn good team. And since I knew show business and he knew plays it made a good working team."[2]

When Names and Junior Whisenhunt returned from the swing in 1941, they were very encouraged. Later that winter, the world was shaken when the Japanese military attacked the American base at Pearl Harbor. The United States immediately declared war on Japan and then Germany declared war on America. The nation geared up immediately for "total war." One of the most immediate questions for most Americans was what the war would cost, especially in terms of the lives that would be lost. Many Americans enlisted immediately, and the American economy felt an immediate surge of activity to supply the weapons and other goods needed to fight a war. The economy had already begun to recover after about 1938 with the threat of war in Europe and its actual outbreak in 1939; now, however, with America in the war, the demands for all kinds of American products increased dramatically.

Both Names and Whisenhunt had served in World War I, but they had become disillusioned about America's role in the struggle. Early on, in his reflections, Whisenhunt decided the war was fought only for the benefit of the rich. The death of his brother in France probably contributed to his attitude. Names had gone through the war without injury, but during the 1920s and 1930s he experienced the same disillusionment that many Americans did about why America fought in that war. During his abortive candidacy for governor of Kansas in 1940, he had written much about war and his opposition to it.

Names and Whisenhunt were both concerned about their oldest sons. They were both under eighteen years of age, but most everyone expected this to be a long war, and it might still be under way when they became old enough to serve.[3]

With the war now a fact, Names and Whisenhunt moved quickly to get back on the road. Maurine and the Names children returned. Her husband, Slim, was with them some of the time, but he often went back to a town in Oklahoma where he was known and worked as a mechanic. When the show was close enough he would come to visit on weekends. The only member of the Whisenhunt family who was to travel with the show was Junior Whisenhunt. Bill Whisenhunt was going to stay with the pool hall, his wife had no interest in traveling, and the other three children were considered too young to travel, even though the Names children had traveled with the show when they were that age and younger.

Those plans changed slightly just as America entered the war and Whisenhunt's pool hall closed. This was a blow to Whisenhunt since he expected good business with improving cotton prices, and he had planned to make money from the pool hall to supplement whatever he made from the show. Now, suddenly at loose ends and with no other prospects, he decided to travel with the show himself.

Junior Whisenhunt and his father had a trailer house or "house car" built to use on the show. A local Meadow man, Tom Mitchell, found the chassis of a truck or a trailer and used it for the base upon which he built the wooden trailer. It was quite small, probably not more than fifteen feet long, but it was a place to sleep and cook meals. It had no bathroom and only a hot plate for cooking. Junior was very proud of his new home on wheels. He had an old car with which he pulled the trailer.[4]

Whisenhunt soon realized that the show was doing well and more transportation was needed. Names had an old International truck, but it was not large enough to haul all the equipment needed for the operation. When it was loaded and moving down the highway, it was piled so high with young boys riding on the top that it resembled the truck belonging to the Joads in *The Grapes of Wrath*. Whisenhunt returned to Meadow and bought a 1938 bobtail Ford truck. It was in good condition and relieved the pressure on Art's antiquated six-wheel truck, a vehicle that was quite old and sometimes had to be coaxed along. Since Names was never sure it would make it up even small hills, the boys would be ordered off the top while it labored up the grades, and sometimes they pushed it to help it up hills. Despite its age and cranky nature, the truck continued to serve the show for the length of the Whisenhunt-Names partnership. When the show was packed for moving, both trucks were totally loaded down.

Names pulled his housecar behind his truck, Junior Whisenhunt pulled his trailer behind his car, Maurine had a trailer house and car that she drove, and Whisenhunt had his truck. The show was a small caravan moving from town to town.[5]

Names decided to use Meadow as the base of operation and to make a circuit that would go north and return to Meadow for the winter. He decided to play towns where he was known—where he had played before—and, true to his previous practice, stayed away from large communities. He considered a town of five thousand or more people to be large, and many of the towns he played were less than one thousand in population. This was a good strategy, mostly because he had a reputation in those towns and there would be little competition from other forms of entertainment.

The show started out from Meadow in the spring and went in a generally northern direction into the Texas panhandle. The troupe might leave as early as March, but the weather was still pretty cold at that time. Certainly, by April or May, the caravan would be on the road.[6] Names moved the show to take advantage of the agricultural harvest. In Kansas and eastern Colorado he was aiming for the wheat harvest (and the broomcorn harvest in Colorado) when the farmers would have money and many transient workers would be present to do the harvest. Depending upon the specific circumstances of harvest and the reception of the communities they encountered, the show would move out of Texas and play several towns in the Oklahoma panhandle, then move into Kansas. Sometimes the show would move farther east in Kansas, sometimes as far as McCracken.[7]

Late in the season in 1942, the show played Names's hometown of Mc-Cracken for one night only on August 31. The local newspaper was very happy that Names was returning home and gave the show a good buildup and then a good review. The editor said that Names's three sons were now doing much of the acting and that they were very good. He said, "Those who have seen Art's show this season say that the boys are exceptionally clever and interesting." The company was going to present "this year's super-sensation, 'Deep in the Heart of Texas.' This is a wonderful play, with lots of comedy and plenty of romance and mystery." The paper was also impressed that the admission prices were so low—thirty cents for adults and ten cents for children, plus tax.[8] In the next week's paper, the editor gave a glowing review of everything about the show.[9]

Sometimes the show might cross briefly into Nebraska, but not often. It did go into eastern Colorado on several occasions because in addition to the wheat grown there, eastern Colorado was a good area for broomcorn, which required a large labor force to harvest the specialized corn raised for the making of brooms. Two of the best towns for the show in Colorado were Brush and Kim.

After reaching its most northern point, the show would begin a slow swing back southward so that it would be back in Oklahoma and Texas in time to catch the cotton harvest. Before mechanization, when cotton was pulled by hand, enormous amounts of labor were necessary to bring the cotton in before it could be damaged by the weather. Local residents provided much of the labor, but the lion's share was provided by migrant workers from South Texas, most of whom were Mexican Americans.

Depending on how good business was, the show would stay out as long as it could. Names and Whisenhunt had double-sidewalled the tent to keep out the cold winds, and they had installed portable heaters to keep the interior as warm as they could; but staying on the road all winter was not a desirable goal. The show might return to Meadow by Thanksgiving or it might be closer to Christmas, again depending on how good business was.[10]

When the company returned to Meadow, the tent was set up in winter quarters. The sidewalls were packed at the bottom with dirt to keep out the cold winds, and other weatherproofing that could be done was undertaken. With portable heaters, the interior was reasonably comfortable. During the deep winter months in Meadow, the show would present motion pictures, which did not make a lot of money, but both Names and Whisenhunt thought it best to keep the show open to make whatever they could.

During the Whisenhunt partnership, the show followed two patterns, depending on circumstances and the response of the audiences. One pattern was a three-night stand in a community to play Monday, Tuesday, and Wednesday nights. On Wednesday night the show would be struck after the performance and loaded on to the trucks by daylight the next morning. The caravan would leave as early as possible to move to the next town where the tent would be erected for a performance that night, and the same three plays were presented on Thursday, Friday, and Saturday nights in the new town. After the Saturday night performance, the tent would be struck again and the show would move out early on Sunday to the next town. This move was a bit more leisurely since Names never presented a performance on Sunday night.

Most moves were relatively short. Sometimes the show merely went to the next small town, which might be no more than 20 or 30 miles. "Big jumps," usually more than 50 miles and sometimes as much as 100 or 150 miles, were usually reserved for the weekend move since there was more time. Names tried to move far enough that he would be serving a new audience. As the war continued and prosperity became more widespread, short moves became something of a problem since farmers and small-town residents were buying vehicles and might drive a few miles to see the show. He had to move far enough away that he was not, in fact, competing with himself. Of course, during the war years, this was not a significant problem because after 1942 no American automobiles were produced. Car factories were now producing war materials, and the rationing of gasoline and rubber greatly restricted the distances people could drive, especially for pleasure.[11]

When the show was playing three-night stands, the plays were always the same. The first night Names would present *Are You a Monkey?*, a play about Darwinian evolution he had written in the 1920s soon after the Scopes trial. It was one of his most successful plays, which he had presented in many different formats over the years. Even people who had seen it before came back because it had been several years since Names had been to their town and because it was a popular play. The second night the company presented *Deep in the Heart of Texas*, which was billed as a new play but actually was a rewritten and renamed play that Names had used many times in the past. It proved to be very popular in most of the towns they played, especially when Maurine's new husband, Slim, played the romantic lead. The third night, Names would present a play he called *Toby's Ghost*, one of the many "Toby" plays presented by most rep companies. These plays were clever farces and good notes on which to close.

The second pattern was to play a week in a town, especially when the community was considered a good town for the show. On these occasions, new plays had to be learned and rehearsed since Names did not present any of the three plays done on the three-night stands. Names could sometimes be a bit erratic, as Milburn Stone had said of Names's earliest days when he might decide to present a different play with a warning of only a day or two. This could present problems with so many teenage actors who sometimes were not the most diligent in learning lines, and especially if they had never performed the play before. But, as he told Stone, Names believed people could do almost anything. When a new play was being presented for the first time, there were sometimes some awkward moments, but most of the time the actors were able to present a credible performance, even when they were improvising a bit.[12]

The traveling tent show was an efficient operation. Names had honed the process over the years, and with Whisenhunt it worked perfectly. The tent was ragged and patched, but it was functional, and Names kept working on it all

the time to keep it as attractive as possible. In 1944 the business was successful enough that Names and Whisenhunt bought an extension that made the
tent more than 100 feet long; one participant said it was 50 feet wide and 140
feet long.[13] They bought a used tent and placed it and the old tent together
end to end. They also bought a new sidewall that went completely around the
enlarged tent, making it a double sidewall all the way around.[14] The tent had
center poles and side poles that kept it elevated.

When the show arrived in a town, it always attracted a crowd of boys and
young men. Names engaged several of them by distributing free passes to do
much of the labor of erecting the tent. The tent top was spread out on the
ground, places were marked for stakes, stakes were driven, and guy ropes
were tied loosely. The most difficult job was to raise the center poles, which
were square and thirty or so feet in length. Holes were drilled about three feet
from the bottom of the poles, and on the other end were steel bars embedded
in the end of the poles. Workers crawled under the tent on the ground and
worked their way to the center poles, where they placed the steel bar through
the hole in the top of the tent. Then three or four persons under the tent top
would get on each side of the pole and grasp a steel rod, often an axle from
an old car, and together they would push the pole, with someone guiding it,
up in the air. With sheer strength they would push the pole all the way and
stand it up while other workers would tighten the guy ropes on the outside to
the stakes that had been driven earlier. The process would be repeated for
each of the center poles, usually three or four, depending on the length of the
tent. Once all center poles were standing, the crew went around the tent from
stake to stake, adjusting the tension on the ropes so that the top of the tent
was properly anchored down without any strain on any part of it. Then the
side poles, about six or seven feet tall placed every few feet around the edge
of the tent to hold the top canvas off the ground, were raised. The last step
for the tent was to install the sidewalls. The side canvas was attached to the
edge of the tent top at regular intervals. After the double sidewall was purchased by Names and Whisenhunt, the workers regularly stretched the side
canvas around the tent twice.[15]

The seating, of which Names usually had two types, was installed before
the sidewalls were put in place, mostly because it was easier for workers to
walk in and out of the tent all around and it was cooler for the workers in the
hot summer days of the plains. In the front part of the audience, folding
wooden chairs were placed to serve as reserved seats that cost a few cents
more. In the back were bleacher-type seats that were dismantled and stacked

for moving after the performance. Some people believed that Names invented the structure of the bleacher seats, but others thought this style was common in tent shows.

Once the tent was in place, the stage was the next to be installed. The tent had one end that was left open, where Names's old International truck was driven so that the side of the truck faced the inside of the tent. The sideboard of the truck was reinforced and hinged so that it could be laid down parallel with the ground and placed on large timbers that had been cut for that purpose. The side of the truck was leveled and stabilized so that it could handle the sets and several people at one time. This was the stage. The other side of the truck bed remained upright and became the back wall of the stage. A special piece of canvas had been cut so that it fit around the installed stage and hooked to the sides of the tent.

Once the stage was installed and the end of the tent was enclosed, the next step was to install the stage set, curtains, and backstage areas. The scenery was all hanging cloth since Names had no wooden flats usually found in indoor theaters. The back and sides of the sets were cloth or canvas, painted with various scenes for the particular plays. Often the back and sides were painted to simulate the walls of a room and included windows painted on the cloth, but wooden doors with floor hooks were installed where necessary. The front curtain was suspended from the top and rolled up and down, not to the sides as was common in most indoor theaters. The front curtain could be dropped much faster than side curtains could be closed, something quite important for blackout scenes. Actually, the front curtain was hung this way because it was easier to mount at the top than to pull it from the sides.

In front of the curtain was a row of footlights mounted on the edge of the stage and pointed at the performing area. The lights had special backing to direct the light and keep the glare out of the audience's eyes. These lights were simple electric light bulbs; their main purpose was to get light on the stage at the lower levels. Theatrical lights were hung above the curtain line on the stage and were adjusted for the demands of the play.[16]

At different times during the life of the Names show, several types of box offices were utilized. During the Whisenhunt partnership, a small square wooden box office, which was hinged and folded flat for traveling, was installed at one corner on the front of the tent. It had a window and a shelf so that the person selling tickets could work efficiently. Next to the box office was a wooden door mounted in the front sidewall that was hinged to open to the inside of the tent.

Refreshment income was important to the company, and the refreshment stand was inside the tent at the front where the patrons would be tempted as they entered. During the Whisenhunt partnership, concessions were limited to popcorn and snow cones, which were sold all during the performances. The salt water taffy was sold only between acts.[17]

The trailer houses were located on the lot fairly close to the tent, creating something of a compact community or compound for the show people. The trailers were close to the tent because the teenage boys slept in the tent on folding army-type cots since no room was available in the trailers; they also provided a measure of security since someone was always in the tent, day and night. Because none of the trailer houses had bathrooms, the occupants used chamber pots in the evenings. Maurine and Beulah Whisenhunt, when she visited, used chamber pots in the daytime as well. In most towns, there were no real facilities available, and the male crew members dug holes not far away from the trailers. In the mornings someone would empty the chamber pots, or, as they called them, "slop jars," into the holes. Art regularly carried out the slop jar from Maurine's trailer when her husband was not there. During the night the boys sleeping in the tent would use the outdoors for bathroom facilities, and sometimes they would dig small holes for latrines that they would cover with small amounts of dirt when they were finished.[18] Jack remembered that when fire destroyed the tent in 1944 in Muleshoe, Texas, "the last thing I threw on the fire was the slop jar."[19]

Maurine Names had always been well known for her appearance in towns where the show played. She had long curls when she was younger, reminiscent of the young Shirley Temple, and when she was older her hair was still very stylish and kept in tight curls. No one ever remembered seeing her when her hair was not perfect. Maurine said sometimes women in some of the towns accused her of wearing wigs, even though she never wore one, and a few times women tried to pull the wig from her head, making her head quite sore. She apparently did her own hair and stayed indoors anytime it was in curlers or did not look its best.[20]

Maurine was also famous for her clothes. The men wore costumes that fit the parts, sometimes tuxedos or business suits, or working men's clothes if they were appropriate. Maurine, on the other hand, always wore costumes of the latest fashions and sometimes seemed overdressed for the parts. When she was asked if she had costumes made, she said that she almost never had anything made and bought the clothing she needed. For a few special plays, she deliberately bought outfits from stores, and, on one occasion, she ordered a wedding outfit from Paris. She said, "I spent a lot of money on them. I hardly ever bought anything for street use."[21]

Once the tent was up and the troupe got some rest, the next item of business was to do advance work in the next town. A few members of the company, usually Names, Whisenhunt, and one or two of the boys, would drive to the next town on the show itinerary. Names would make arrangements for a vacant lot, electricity, and licenses if any were needed. Because Names was known in most of the towns they played, he usually received a warm welcome, but periodically a city official would try to take advantage of the situation and charge outrageous license fees, either to make money for the town or to keep the company away. Seldom was Names unable to overcome such obstacles.

The advance team would go to stores and vacant buildings where they placed advertising for the show. Some of Names's advertising was the same that circuses used. With different one-sheets (as they were called) and individual sheets for days of the week and others for numbers, the posters could be made for the specific time the show would be in town. In this way it was not necessary to print special one-sheets for each town although Names did have some special posters made for some of the plays, especially *Are You a Monkey?*, which had a blank space at the bottom where the town and date could be written in. Names usually gave free passes to businessmen who allowed his advertising in the store windows. In fact, Names gave so many passes that Whisenhunt sometimes was bothered by his generosity. Names always justified it by saying it was better to build goodwill than to insist on charging for admission. Names also said that many of the passes given out would not be used, and even if they were, the company would probably make more from concession sales to these people than they would from admission. Names was correct about some of the businesses not using the passes, but they could be assured that the passes given to boys and young men for their work in erecting the tent would be used.[22] One troupe member remembered Names being so kindhearted that he would give passes to children who did not have any money; it seemed he would keep no one out, "but if he caught kids sneaking in, then he was tough on them."[23]

When the company was ready to move after a stay in a town, the show was packed up in record time. There was a definite routine for striking the tent, and when it was followed carefully, everything went smoothly. During the early days, Names had roughnecks who did all the work, but during the Whisenhunt partnership everything—labor, acting, advertising, and so forth—was done by the same people.

The stage was dismantled by packing all the drapery, scenery, stage furniture, stage lights, curtains, and everything on the stage into places that had been designed for each piece. Wardrobes were used to store costumes and makeup and were loaded on the bed of the truck. Then the seats were folded or dismantled and loaded onto the truck while it was still under the end of the tent; then the sidewalls would be removed, folded, and put into the truck. At that point, someone would pull the truck out from the end of the tent and the tent top would be dropped. One of the crew remembered that they "could drop the tent in just a few minutes. There was a real routine for packing." Once everything was loaded into the two trucks, the show was ready to move out. The loading could be done in a couple of hours, and the show would be ready to move by midnight or one o'clock in the morning.

The show might pull out immediately if the next move was a "long jump," or the crew might take the opportunity to sleep a few hours before daylight and then move out in the morning. This was a bit difficult for the young boys who normally slept in the tent and would have to improvise if they waited until daylight to move. Most of the time, Names was ready to go, and he would try to get the show out of the town as soon as possible. Even if the show moved out before daylight, Names made it a point to wait until mid-morning or so to arrive in the next town. If necessary, the caravan might stop along the road somewhere to rest and wait for the next day since Names knew he should arrive in the next community after the town was awake and people were on the streets. In this way, his company was like a circus. He did not have a parade—although in the early days, he had a band that played as the company entered a town. During the Whisenhunt period, they had none of these extras, but Names wanted people to see the caravan arrive because he knew it would attract a crowd and there would be plenty of young men to help erect the tent. The entrance into a town was sometimes the best advertising the show got, and it certainly helped create interest in the first night's show.

Usually, the show arrived in a town early enough to erect the tent by early afternoon. That gave the crew time to rest and for the word-of-mouth advertising to spread around town. Names would spend much time during the day walking up and down the main street of the small town, greeting old friends and making new ones. He was quite a mixer and engendered trust and respect.[24]

Attending a performance of the Art Names Show was an experience that most people never forgot. It was not spectacular as a circus or carnival was, nor was it educational as the Chautauqua was. It was a small, two-family operation that brought some excitement and wholesome entertainment to a rural audience not often exposed to professional theater.

When people approached the tent on the way to a performance, they were probably already quite familiar with the large tent sitting on a vacant lot in the center of town where it could not be missed. Even so, pulses must have quickened as the lights outside the tent became visible and the colorful box office came into sight. Playgoers approached the box office and were greeted by Whisenhunt in a courteous way or, if Names were there, as if they were old friends or family. To pay thirty cents for adults and nine cents for children for admission was a major expense for most rural people in the late 1930s and early 1940s—a time when the price of an adult admission might equal, or almost equal, an hour's wage.

They entered the tent through a wooden door set in a frame and placed in the end or corner of tent. Inside, playgoers were confronted with a typical theater arrangement. At the end of the tent was the stage with a heavy cloth curtain covering it. Lights on the stage were minimal at this time.

The whole operation was a bit tattered and worn. Today it might be considered rundown, but at the time, it had a lot of dignity despite its condition. Much of that dignity came from the personality of Names.

The inside of the tent usually provided a festive atmosphere. As in any theater before a performance, there was a sense of anticipation. The canvas theater was something different, and the smell of canvas was distinctive. Usually the crew had used water hoses to sprinkle the ground inside the tent before the performance to keep down the dust. This also gave the inside a slightly moist or humid feel. With the canvas and slightly wet smell, the inside of the tent was an atmosphere quite different from anything most of the audience had seen before.

As the playgoers walked down the aisle, they would choose their seats. If they had been willing to pay an extra ten cents they could use the reserved seats at the front of the theater. These were wooden folding chairs. If they had not been willing to pay the extra amount, they would take their seats on the grandstand-like wooden benches in the back of the theater. Except for the comfort of sitting on the ground on a regular chair, there was little difference between the two types of seating. Audience members in either place could see and hear the performance clearly.

As the people entered the tent, they found a popcorn machine to the side of the entrance. It was flanked by an ice-shaving mechanism used to make snow cones. Shaved ice was put in a funnel-type cup and covered with a sweet syrup for flavoring. Popcorn was also sold in a funnel-type container that was a bit deceptive in appearance. It seemed to be a fairly large portion because it was tall, but actually the containers did not hold very much because it became so small at the bottom end. Now a decision had to be made. Would limited funds be used for this food or would it be saved for purchasing candy between acts? Popcorn and snow cones were five cents each. For one person that might not be much, but if a family came, admission and food could add up to a substantial sum.

At the appropriate time, the house lights would dim as the footlights came on. Art Names would step from backstage and stand in front of the closed curtain. Today, this is usually called a warm-up, a time to get the audience loosened up and ready for the performance. Names would welcome the audience and tell them how good their town was to him and how he always wanted to come back year after year. He was just a neighbor to many people, an old friend welcoming them. Then Names usually would recite a poem. Sometimes he recited his own work and other times he used well-known poetry that was a proven audience pleaser. Names had the voice to make the poetry entertaining no matter what it was. When he finished his greetings, he announced the play and stepped behind the curtain.

Names had tried to increase the anticipation for the play to come, and it usually worked. As the curtain was raised, there was a hush over the audience as the first action began.

At the end of the acts the curtain usually dropped very fast in a blackout manner. This cut the play abruptly and shook the audience back to reality. The footlights would dim and the house lights came up. Now it was time to sell candy.

The saltwater taffy sales were a major source of income for the show. Each box cost the customer ten cents; it usually had three or four pieces of candy inside. As an enticement, Names placed coupons in some of the boxes to be redeemed for prizes that were displayed on stage. Entertainment of various types, mostly vaudeville, was provided during the intermission as the candy sales went on. The intermission lasted as long as anyone was buying candy. As the end of the next act the candy sales occurred again.

At the end of the production, the playgoers most often left feeling good about the experience. They may have been to Names's show before; they may even have seen the same play before. They may have thought the plays were "corny" or they may have considered them serious drama. In any case, almost all the people who attended a Names show left without feeling they had been shortchanged in any way.

Junior Whisenhunt was the only member of the Whisenhunt family to act for some time. His enthusiasm for the show was overflowing, and his optimism and enthusiasm were infectious. Some thirty years or more later, two members of the Names family remembered Junior's first appearance on the stage with humor and affection. In his first performance, in which he was to portray a prominent businessman, Maurine said she checked him over "to see if he was okay. And darn if he didn't have on a pair of cowboy boots and one pant's leg hiked up over the top." She really scolded him about wearing the boots, telling him he was supposed to be a millionaire New Yorker and "he had these cowboy boots on just pure Texas style." After Junior Whisenhunt was killed in World War II, Maurine said, "After what happened I felt real bad about that because I thought, now that is just pure Texas." As she looked back, she said, "I think that's a sweet memory." She said he was a real trouper and "took to the drama real good. He liked drama. And he took directions good too because he would try and he'd try and he'd try. But he really liked it. Nineteen, I think he was nineteen when he started doing that."[25] Jack Names, one of the twins, well remembered Junior's wearing cowboy boots. His response was, "Well, hell, we didn't have much else to wear, let's face it."[26]

Life on the road, a unique experience for the Whisenhunt family, was something quite familiar to the Names family. Yet few people in America experienced such a way of life. Traveling shows of many types existed, of course, but the great majority of Americans lived in the same place for long periods of time. Even though America is known as a mobile society and many families move two or three times during their lifetimes, that does not mean that they are nomadic as are the traveling entertainment shows, whether they are circuses, repertory shows, carnivals, medicine shows, or even religious tent-revival operations.

Back home in Meadow, Texas, the Whisenhunt children were the envy of most of the young people they knew. Their friends' parents were not necessarily as enthralled with the idea of life on the road, even if most of them did like Art Names and trusted that if anyone could lead a seminormal life when he moved every week or more often, then Art Names could do it. Friends of the Whisenhunt children thought of the experience they were involved in as very romantic and exciting; because the country had been in such a serious depression for so long, many young people could not remember anything other than hard times. Now their friends were having the experience of a lifetime, going from town to town and performing every night on the stage.[27]

The new Art Names Show had some serious problems, mostly related to the new world war. Everyone understood that this was a fight for survival; the fascists of Europe—Hitler and Mussolini—and the militarists of Japan would not settle short of total victory. Americans assumed that the Allied goal would be "unconditional surrender" even though that policy was not formally declared until the Casablanca Conference of 1943.

The most serious problem faced by the show, and by civilians of all sorts, was the wartime rationing that went into effect soon after the war started. With the Japanese moving across the Pacific and dislodging European colonial powers, some vital raw materials, such as rubber, sugar, and petroleum, were under the control of the Japanese. The American government instituted domestic rationing to conserve the limited supplies available of these and other raw materials. For example, everyone was assigned a rationed amount of gasoline per week or per month based on the occupation of the person. Physicians who made house calls and those who traveled for a living received more gallons per week than an average person. The government agencies involved were quite strict in their interpretation of essential occupations, and Names and Whisenhunt had some difficulty in getting enough ration stamps to buy the gasoline they needed.

The same problems existed with rubber, but in some ways it was more intense since the United States did not produce any rubber at all. Most of the rubber used in the past had come from colonial areas now controlled by Japan. A crash program was inaugurated to develop synthetic rubber, but it took some time for the process to be perfected, and the first synthetic rubber was not very good quality. The same situation existed with sugar, which was critical for concessions, especially snow cones, since many of the nation's previous suppliers were no longer available.[28]

The story of shortages during World War II is well known. As will normally happen, an active black market in ration stamps or coupons developed for the various products, but there is no evidence that Names and Whisenhunt participated. Names, because he was known and liked by so many of the people in the towns they played, was able to beg and borrow some of the scarce items they needed. For example, a man from Booker, Texas, remembered, as mentioned earlier, how he gave some worn-out tires to Names. One way or the other, the show got what it needed and survived the scarcities of the war years.[29]

The response the Names-Whisenhunt operation received from people in local communities was generally quite good. As the show moved from town to town, many people came to see Names and his former wife to welcome them back to their town. They commented on how they had attended the show in earlier years and had wondered about Names during the hard Depression years. Most of them were pleased to know that he had survived and now was back on the road with a full-scale live stage show.

One thing Names did to keep in touch with the people was to go every morning very early to the local café, the major one in town, if there were more than one. He would sit at the counter, drink five or six cups of coffee, and read the morning paper. People often interrupted him, and he was happy to talk with them; Names was a real conversationalist. This was one of the ways that Names was able to make the people in the towns recognize that he was just like them, not some pompous, ego-driven actor who had to have special treatment.[30]

There were times, of course, when relations with locals soured. Often, that had to do with misunderstandings or excessive drinking by some of the townspeople. On one occasion, a serious problem occurred during a performance in Kim, Colorado, when a man and his son, both drunk, caused a disturbance in the audience. Names tried from the stage to calm the man down and keep him quiet, and he finally went down into the audience and confronted the man but could not convince him to be quiet. Names's son, Jack, remembered the incident very well and recalled, "I have never known Dad to hit anybody else in my life, but he clobbered this old man who was about his age, and, of course, that put the old man out of commission." The son was in his twenties. He hit Names, blacking his eye and cutting him up badly. Names did not expect any help when the audience pushed the chairs back and formed a circle. Jack Names ran down the center aisle and dove over two rows of chairs and hit the son, knocking him to the ground. He was pretty drunk, and Jack was able to hold him down. Just as the man tried to hit Jack, his twin brother, Jean, stomped on the young man's fingers, and the two of them held him down and stopped the fight. When Names was able to get the audience back in place, Jack Names made a joke from the stage, and the tension was broken. Kenneth Whisenhunt said he could not remember Names ever losing his temper, but when he heard the story, he said he had forgotten that incident.[31]

When people attended a Names show, they could count on several things, one of which was that Names would recite a poem before the performance. Sometimes he recited one of his own poems, sometimes works by popular

TENT SHOW

poets such as John W. Service. Names occasionally recited "The Shooting of Dan McGrew" and "The Cremation of Sam McGee." Whisenhunt thought he did not like to recite these two poems because they were so long, but Maurine recalled that he did not like to recite long poems because he would get lost in the recitation. She said, "He'd get to wandering around, you know, and he'd get lost. I've seen Art get so lost that he'd have to start all over again."[32]

Candy, popcorn, and snow cones were the staple products sold before the show started. Most of the time, the Whisenhunt children, Kenneth and Lewis, operated the concessions, but, if needed, one of the twins would help out.[33] Between acts, a major activity was to sell boxes of saltwater taffy in boxes similar to Cracker Jack boxes containing three or four pieces of taffy. Maurine said the taffy was not of very high quality, but seldom did anyone complain. Between acts the stage set could be changed if necessary, but the major objective was to sell candy and provide short between-acts entertainment, most of it vaudeville-style comedy that consisted of one-liners between two people on stage, usually Art and one of his sons. They would use vaudeville blackouts, but since the cast was so small and none of them had musical ability, real vaudeville entertainment—song and dance—could not be provided. Mostly, the entertainment was corny jokes to keep the people occupied while the candy sellers went among the patrons. Names sometimes used magic or other sleight-of-hand activities to entertain.

One of his most popular stunts was the never-empty bowl. He would take a small pot or bowl to the edge of the stage, pour water out, and show the audience that the pot was completely empty of water. Other things would go on for a while, and then Art would take the pot to the edge of the stage and again pour out water. The audience could not understand how it had water in it, since he had already emptied it. He would repeat this two or three times. It was so intriguing to the audience that there was always water in the pot that someone always stayed around after the performance to find out how this trick worked. Names would never tell, and he would not let anyone see the pot. The secret was that the inside of the pot was lined with cork that was porous and would hold water. Before the stunt, Names would fill the pot and let the cork soak up as much water as it would. As the pot sat on the table between each time it was emptied, water would leak from the cork and some would be available to pour out each time. This was a simple device, but it kept the people entertained between acts.[34]

Names added prizes to the boxes of candy to entice people to buy. During the day, he would type slips of paper with the name of a prize on it and put them in the boxes. He bought carnival type prizes, such things as ashtrays, glass bowls, trinkets, and small stuffed animals, but the main attractions were large stuffed teddy bears. Names would put the prizes on tables on the stage between acts and hang several of the teddy bears on the curtain to entice people to buy. He got the candy from a wholesaler in cartons of 36 or 48 boxes. When the candy was sold, people who had one of the slips would take it to the stage and Names would make a big announcement as he gave the person the prize. Names promised that in each carton of candy there was at least one box that contained a slip for the large teddy bear.

Kenneth Whisenhunt vividly remembered selling candy. Kenneth and the Names twins sold candy most of the time, but later, Whisenhunt's third son, Lewis, joined the sales crew. The boys received a 10 percent commission on sales, which sold for ten cents per box. Kenneth Whisenhunt told of how receptive the towns were in Colorado during the broomcorn harvest. Business was so good in one town that the show moved on to the next town that already had been visited by the advance team, but as soon as that engagement was finished the show moved back to the previous town. Business was as good or better on the second visit. This was one of the occasions when new plays had to be learned quickly so the troupe would not repeat itself in the first town.

Kenneth Whisenhunt said that the people working in the harvest had money and were willing to spend it. The broomcorn harvesters, known as "Broomcorn Johnnies," were willing to spend their money, especially on girlfriends. He told about several times when one of the "Johnnies" would call him over, tell him to dump all the boxes of candy on the ground, and buy all the boxes, determined to get one of the large teddy bears for his girlfriend. He and his girlfriend would then go through the boxes until they found the one with the coupon. Kenneth remembered that he and the other boys sold three or four hundred dollars' worth of candy in one night. Candy sales of $350 would equal 100 to 150 admissions to the show, and 10 percent commission on that amount was significant income for the teenage boys.[35]

Bill Whisenhunt mostly sold tickets and helped with the refreshments. Since the popcorn machine was located near the box office at the entrance to the tent, he kept enough popcorn ready for the crowd. His sons would help with the popcorn and snow cones before the performance and would sell the taffy between acts.

Even though Whisenhunt did not act, there was one play in which he appeared. The script called for a dead body to lie at the back of the stage during a long period, and Whisenhunt was willing to play dead on stage since he said that did not require any talent. One night while he was pretending to be a corpse the other actors on the stage were firing pistols. Even though the bullets were blanks, fire came from the barrels of the pistols, and one of the shots caught the scenery on fire. Because the fire was near Whisenhunt's head where he was lying as a corpse, he saw the fire when no one else did. Kenneth recalled, "He just reached up and patted his hands together to put the fire out."[36]

One of the potentially destructive problems the traveling tent show faced on the Great Plains of the United States was weather, particularly tornadoes in the summer months. Kansas, Oklahoma, and the Texas panhandle are so prone to tornadoes that some parts of the region have been called "tornado alley." Clearly, a tent is vulnerable to all kinds of weather problems, but especially to storms with high winds.

Throughout his career, Names had his show damaged numerous times by high winds and tornadoes. On one occasion in a Kansas town, the show was hit by an unexpected storm while almost everyone was gone to the next town doing advance work. When the group had left, the weather was clear and there was no forecast of trouble. During the middle of the afternoon, a storm blew in unexpectedly, with strong winds and heavy rain. The ropes that hold the tent to the stakes have to be adjusted during a storm because wet canvass contracts and stretches, and, if the ropes remain taut, the tent can be stretched too tight. The ropes can break and sections of the tent top can blow out if there is too much pressure on the tent. Sometimes, if the wind is too strong, some of the stakes may pull out of the ground, causing more trouble. To protect a tent during a storm, people must move around adjusting ropes, driving stakes, and generally working in the storm to see that the tent does not get full of wind and blow away.

On this occasion almost everyone was gone. Whisenhunt's wife and their youngest son, Donald, were on one of their occasional visits. Neither she nor the young son, who was about four or five years old, would be any help in a storm. The only two members of the troupe in town were Maurine and Lewis Whisenhunt, the third son of Bill Whisenhunt, who was about fourteen or fifteen years old, too young, most would assume, to be able to help protect the tent.

But, as the storm raged, Maurine and Lewis did everything anyone else would have done had they been present. They moved around the tent adjusting ropes, driving stakes, and watching for wind getting under the tent. The storm was a fairly short one, but for two people it was exhausting. Both

ON THE ROAD AGAIN

of them worked as hard as they could, and when the storm passed, the tent was still standing. Lewis was so tired, he was shaking. Wet and dirty, Maurine was certainly not the glamorous actress that most people knew, with her normally perfect hair hanging down in her face.

Names and Whisenhunt said that on their drive back, they could see the storm cloud and were fairly certain that it was hitting the town where the tent was. They assumed that the tent would be a total loss and were making plans for how they would pay for replacing it. Their surprise was obvious when they drove up and found the tent intact. An inspection found only two small rips in the canvas, and Names could not believe that only the two of them had saved the tent. Names gave Lewis Whisenhunt five dollars for his efforts. Maurine remembered the storm vividly. She said that she often helped out in storms to keep the tent on the ground and that "Art said he would rather leave me with the tent in a storm and be sure that it would be up than he would with most roughnecks."[37]

Another time, also in a Kansas town, a storm blew in just about curtain time. The tent was already partially filled, but the clouds had looked threatening, and many people had decided to stay home rather than risk danger by going to the show. Before the performance could begin, the storm hit with full force, and local residents scattered while the troupe tried to save the tent.

Whisenhunt's wife and youngest son were visiting on this occasion as well. Whisenhunt took his wife and son to the truck that served as stage, and they crawled under the truck, where they were probably as safe as they could be anywhere in this situation. The Names and Whisenhunt families spent the rest of the storm trying to save the tent, but this time they were not so fortunate. The wind was strong, the rain was hard, the tent became taut, and sections of the tent top began to blow out. The top of the tent was a series of ropes made in squares, and between the squares were large sections of canvas. Some of these sections could pop out fairly easily when the wind got under the tent. Several times some of the teenage boys could be seen running across vacant lots and into fields with growing crops chasing sections of canvas. When the storm ended, the tent was still standing, but it was mostly a skeleton of ropes, most of the canvas sections having blown out. Some of the seating inside the tent had been damaged, but all in all the damage could have been much worse.

Though the tent was unusable in its present condition, Names was not one to be discouraged. He told Whisenhunt that he had endured much worse on other occasions, and they needed only to make a few repairs. He assured Whisenhunt they would be in business again. The next day, when the weather was nice again, the pieces of the tent were gathered up, the seating was removed, and the skeleton of the tent was dropped to the ground. All members of the troupe began to sew by hand the canvas sections back to the ropes that held them in place. Several days were required before the work was done, but then the tent was functional again. It was a bit worse for the wear and was a patched operation, but it was watertight and protected the audiences. This was a setback, but it was not disastrous. Names liked to say that he had been totally destroyed in previous storms, but Whisenhunt was not as nonchalant and continued to worry about future problems, wondering if he had done the right thing by getting into this business.[38] Jean Names remembered two storms particularly. He said, "Nothing could be as frightening as being inside one of those tents with the tent flopping up and down like that and feeling all the elements really expanded. If you were outside, the rain would be a whole lot calmer than trying to hold down that tent. That thing flopped around with a 15 foot center pole."[39]

One of the most serious blows the show suffered was when the eldest sons of both Names and Whisenhunt joined military service. Art Names, Jr., went first and volunteered for the 101st Airborne—the Paratroopers, one of the elite units of the United States military—and went to Fort Benning, Georgia, for training.[40] Junior Whisenhunt waited a bit longer but eventually volunteered, serving in the infantry. He had gone back to Meadow after the war began and worked for a while on farms in the area. Since agricultural work was considered vital to the war effort, he was able to get a deferment. By about 1943 he told his father he was sure he would be drafted eventually, and he had decided to go ahead and volunteer.[41]

The two boys' departure from the show left a void. The only experienced actors, other than Art and Maurine, were the Names twins, but they were young teenagers who had some difficulty playing mature roles in the various plays. Neither Whisenhunt nor his wife would consider acting, and the company could not afford to employ other actors. Names and Whisenhunt decided to move Kenneth Whisenhunt, the second son, into some of the important roles, and, eventually, he was playing many of the roles that were more challenging than one would expect of such an inexperienced young man. Eventually, the next son, Lewis Whisenhunt, began to act in various parts.[42]

One of the key roles in Names's most successful play, *Are You a Monkey?*, was a character who turned into a monkey after drinking a potion invented by a mad doctor. None of the actors wanted to play the monkey because he had to have full body makeup outside the ragged clothes that he wore. He wore a wig that resembled monkey fur, and the actor's mouth was filled with teeth that resembled those of apes. Jack, at first, played the monkey, but when Art, Jr., went into the army, Jack moved into his part and Kenneth began playing the monkey; later Lewis was moved into that role. This was a natural role for an inexperienced actor since the part had no lines and required only grunts and moving about the stage. Lewis Whisenhunt said that he always dreaded that Art would single him out, as he did several times, to play the beast.[43]

Another way that Names coped with his cast problems was to use his son Jean to play women's roles in at least two plays. In *Are You a Monkey?*, he played a spinster sister of the doctor. In *Deep in the Heart of Texas* the role was the second female character who also had a minor romantic part in the plot. In both instances the characters were spinsters, not very attractive, and not memorable. Jean dressed in a wig with the hair braided down the back, a plain dress, sensible shoes, and glasses. Jean was not pleased about playing the women's roles, but most everyone agreed he was a creditable woman, and he was stuck in the roles.

One of Names's more unusual efforts to innovate and keep the shows fresh involved the decision to have the youngest of Whisenhunt's sons, Donald, who was only about five years old, perform in a play. Names had a play called *Love and Mustard*, a standard melodrama in which a villain is trying to foreclose a mortgage on the property of the heroine. The twins had played the role of the heroine's young nephew before, but by now they were both too old and big to be convincing in the part. Names decided that Donald would be ideal for the part.

Beulah Whisenhunt objected when it was mentioned to her, saying that he was too young and, since he could not read, could not learn the lines. Maurine quickly volunteered to teach him the part verbally. After some discussion, Beulah agreed, and Maurine taught him the lines and blocking as she promised.

During the night of the performance Donald remembered all his lines and missed only two cues. They were minor, and Names, who was playing the villain, was able to cover the mistakes so that the audience never knew. The play was performed only once with Donald in the role, but it was an experience of a lifetime, one that he always remembered despite his young age.[44]

The troupe adjusted to the absence of Art, Jr., and Junior Whisenhunt and continued to operate. With the absence of the two young men, it was difficult for Names to present a wide variety of plays, particularly if the show left a town and then decided to return a week later because of good business. That required an entirely new group of plays for the second run, but, always resourceful, Names was able to adapt with the limited cast that he had.

One example of Names's resourcefulness was his willingness to use his former wife's new husband as an actor. Slim Worthington was an automobile mechanic by trade, but he had suffered through the Depression like most everyone else. When he married Maurine, they had gone to California where she (and perhaps he) tried unsuccessfully to get into motion pictures. He may have been an actor on the Names show before Names fell on hard times and may have met Maurine in that way. Records regarding Worthington are almost nonexistent.

When Maurine went back with the show, Worthington worked at an auto repair shop in Mangum, Oklahoma, in extreme southwestern Oklahoma where he was known. This was a way for him to supplement the income of his wife and yet not be too far away. On weekends when he came to where the show was playing to see his wife, he often performed in plays. The records show that he played the romantic lead in the melodramatic play Names had written, *Deep in the Heart of Texas*, and a prominent role in the ever popular *Are You a Monkey?* Worthington may have worked full-time at different periods during the Names-Whisenhunt partnership; the records are too incomplete to know for sure. Even as a weekend actor, and more if he were full-time, Names was able to solve part of his cast problem with a more mature and experienced actor in the person of Worthington.[45]

Life on the road had its positive and negative effects on the people who traveled. This was a particularly critical issue for the Names children—and to some extent, the Whisenhunt children—who spent many years of their youth traveling from town to town. Schooling for the Names children was erratic at best. Jean remembered that he and his brothers went to school some years a week at a time. He said, "Our parents would never go down with us. We'd go down and introduce ourselves and we'd say 'We're in the show and we'll be here a week.' They would put us in a class. We learned quite a lot from this though." On Friday of that week, the children would check themselves out of school and repeat the process in the next town. Jack recalled that when he and Jean were in high school, Art took them out of school for two years to work on the show, but he quickly added that they went back to school and made up their freshman and sophomore years during one year. One winter when the Names stayed in Meadow, all three Names children attended

ON THE ROAD AGAIN

Meadow schools.[46] A woman from Garden City, Kansas, whose husband taught eighth grade in Jetmore, Kansas, said that Art, Jr., was in her husband's class and that when he got to Jetmore, it was his thirty-second school of the year. She recalled, "He was a good student and mixed quickly with the other students." Art, Jr., stayed in Jetmore for four weeks to complete the year.[47] The kind of life the boys lived is revealed in another letter in the Names papers from the principal of the grade school in Mulvane, Kansas. In September, 1939, he wrote a "To whom this may concern" letter for the boys to take to future schools. He was complimentary of the boys and said, "This is to certify that these three brothers, Arthur, Jack and Jean Names, have been students in the grade schools here at Mulvane, Kansas for one week. They are good lads with natural ability considerably above average. They are good boys and good mixers. Class discussions and tests prove that they can do good school work."[48]

When he was asked if he thought traveling made the boys more cosmopolitan, Jack Names said, "It did. Sometimes we went to school in thirty or forty different schools a year, you know," giving them a much broader view of the world than that of most of the children they encountered. Because they had been to school in Texas and Oklahoma, school officials in California, when they went there in the late 1930s, assumed they were behind normal students and "put us in the lowest segment because, you know, as far as they were concerned all Oklahomans . . . And so we were in the class one week and the teacher realized that we were the sharpest kids in the class and she made us a little bit odious by comparison because she'd say, 'Are you are going to let these kids from Oklahoma beat you?' And so we were moved up to the highest group they had."[49]

School was a constant problem for the Names children, especially the twins, but Jean was able to complete high school after their father's death in 1945, and Jack later earned a high school equivalency in the military. Both of them entered the military just before the war was over, and when they came back from the army, both went to college. Jean got a master's degree and eventually became an instructor at a community college in California; Jack went to medical school and spent much of his career as a pediatrician in Modesto, California. Some people were amazed with their accomplishments, considering their upbringing, but others said they were smart and ambitious and their success was no surprise.[50]

Living on the road for several months each year had its impact on all members of the company, but in different ways. Maurine said since she had been raised in show business she expected life on the road to be somewhat lonely because her parents raised her to stay away from town people. She remembered she was not a mixer: "I knew some people in every town; you can't help that. But I was brought up different." Her experiences were of a different kind of show business, vaudeville "when vaudeville meant something." She attended a few literary meetings with Art since he was a member of the Kansas Authors' Club and was interested in meeting with other writers, but Maurine was not impressed with literary types. "If you think actors are far out and nutty people, you should go to a group of those people."[51]

For Art, life on the road was what he had chosen, and he loved it. He was such a gregarious person who loved to talk that he made friends wherever he went, and they remembered him through the years. Names maintained a lively correspondence with people in various towns where he had played at one time or another, and the limited number of his surviving letters reveal, to some degree, the kind of person he was. Truly, he enjoyed life on the road and all the things he encountered, even if they were unpleasant.

The Whisenhunt boys enjoyed the road most of the time. Junior Whisenhunt, especially, was taken with show business and hoped to have his own operation when World War II was over. Several of his letters to his parents talked about his plans to have a traveling tent show when he came home. He wrote Art often and talked about the same things, especially that he wanted to have a traveling show that would play one-night stands. Art told Bill Whisenhunt that the boy was being overly ambitious, as moving every day was a man-killer and required a show successful enough that it could employ a separate road crew to do the heavy work. He wrote Junior that there had been times in his youth when he had done one-night stands for a while, but it was just too much work.[52] In reality, the traveling stage show was on its way out, and Junior could not have reversed the trend in popular entertainment, even if tragedy had not intervened.

Junior Whisenhunt was an infantry rifleman fighting against the Japanese in the Philippines, where he served in the follow-up detail behind the lines that were regaining the islands, part of an operation assigned to clean out any Japanese stragglers or snipers. On one occasion, he wrote his parents and asked them to see if they could find a pistol and send it to him. He said that the weapons he was issued were not so good for fighting in close quarters. Bill Whisenhunt went to Lubbock and bought a .38 caliber pistol and sent it to his son along with several boxes of ammunition. It seems odd, looking back on this situation, that the U.S. Post Office allowed him to send a firearm and ammunition through the mails. It may have been illegal then, as it is to-day, to send firearms through the mail, but possibly the local postmaster in Meadow simply allowed Whisenhunt to violate postal regulations and mail the weapon. It never made any difference, however, since Junior was killed in action in April, 1945, before the pistol had time to reach him. The pistol was never returned and nothing more was heard of it.

The official notification from the government to Whisenhunt's parents was that he was squatting beside a foxhole in the evening cooking his dinner when a large shell (presumably artillery) landed nearby, killing him.[53] Members of the troupe had worried much about Art, Jr., and Junior Whisenhunt from the time they entered the service. Some of them felt that Art, Jr., was in the most danger because he was a paratrooper who jumped behind enemy lines and took enormous risks, but as it turned out, Junior was the one who paid the price. His death was devastating to his parents. They eventually overcame their grief and were able to go on with their lives, but the cloud of her son's death hung over Junior's mother for the rest of her life. Even though she had three other sons, Junior was the firstborn, and she was never able to get over his loss. All members of the Whisenhunt and Names families were stunned by the loss. Jack Names remembered years later, "God, everyone was scarred by Junior's death, and Art, Jr., was in the paratroopers. We didn't know whether he was going to die—and your brother died."[54]

Junior's younger brothers Kenneth and Lewis remember life on the road fondly. In the years that they traveled, they always knew that it was temporary. Because their father's future with Names was a year-to-year thing, at any time the partnership could end and the boys could go back to Meadow to stay. They enjoyed what they did, but for them it was never really a way of life.[55]

Little is known about Art, Jr.'s later reflections since he was not anxious to be interviewed. The twins, however, were happy to remember the tent-show days and talked freely about that time of their lives. Life on the road was hard in many ways. In addition to the romance of the road, there was much hard work to be done, especially since there were no roughnecks or laborers to do the physical labor. Jack Names remembered it being very hard work. He said, "Each of us was able to throw a sledgehammer just like grown men. We could handle sledgehammers like you wouldn't believe." They had to drive many stakes in the ground when the tent was erected, and stakes had to be replaced and adjusted from time to time. Jack said, "We could drive stakes together, two of us drive a stake with one on one side and one on the other." They developed a rhythm in this task, with one person hitting the stake while the other was winding up to swing again. This required enormous coordination and trust in the other person wielding a sledgehammer. Jack added, "We could even, at times, drive stakes with one hand. We had muscles enough. We were using eight-pound sledgehammers then."[56]

Relations with town people, according to the twins, were sometimes good but sometimes left something to be desired. Jack said, "Yeah, the town people frequently were against us and sometimes they were for us." Jean agreed: "There's you and there's the townspeople. I recall as a child that there were two distinct societies; one was show people who took care of themselves." The yell "Hey Rube!" was a universal call for help used by all traveling shows—carnivals, circuses, stage shows, and others—a true mark of their separation from the town people.[57] The show people faced the same mixed reaction in the small towns as any other traveling groups would have. Names was well known and trusted by most of the people the show encountered, but there was still some suspicion. The sudden appearance in small towns of four to six teenage boys whose way of life had a romantic attraction to the young people of the towns, especially the girls, could cause resentment among the town boys and anxiety for the town parents.

Jack Names and Kenneth Whisenhunt remembered several occasions in various towns when local girls would hang around the tent and become a problem for the tent show. They recalled a time when a teenage girl in one town seemed to be at the tent night and day and followed them wherever they went. Every day they were in town, the boys went swimming in a lake near town, and when they took off all their clothes for swimming, the girl would sit on a small hill and watch them. Kenneth remembered that she really had a crush on Art, Jr., and wanted to date him.[58]

Events of this sort were not uncommon. To the young people of small towns, the boys on the show represented excitement, mystery, and adventure— even if the impressions were inaccurate. Jack recalled, "We were all in sort of a combination of being looked down on by some of the people and then looked up to as a hero-worship kind of thing and an idealized thing by other people."[59] Just how much contact the boys had with town girls is not clear since the Names and Whisenhunt boys remembered their experiences a bit differently. Kenneth believed that the Names boys, especially Art, Jr., dated a lot of girls. Jack recalled that Names periodically called all the boys to the trailer house and gave them lectures on venereal diseases, even though he was not sure what they were doing; in some ways he was ahead of his time by providing warnings to the boys. Jack said that his father also would warn them from time to time to be wary of girls who were what today would be called "groupies." He remembered a girl in one of the towns who had a crush on him and wrote him letters for some time. "Dad warned me against this type of woman, you know, saying that she was probably a little bit mentally unstable; she must have been crazy." The other boys, both Names and Whisenhunt, had some relationships with town girls, but probably not as much as some people might expect. Jean Names said they were almost always alone, actually, and Jack agreed.[60]

Jack could "remember occasions when people actually came into the tent looking for one of us because their daughter was out with somebody else and because the show was in town; well, it had to be the kids on the show who had taken their daughter out and attacked her or something, you know, and here she was out with some town guy. That happened on a few different occasions."[61] Jack said they actually had few dates with town girls and mostly worked hard even though what they did might have appeared glamorous. Jack recalled, "That was just like living in the goddamn monk's place. Yeah, no dating or anything. Gosh, once in a while maybe once in a blue moon there would be some girls waiting for us after we got the tent all packed and ready to move."

Jack also recalled how people were concerned about the boys. "Many times, not just two or three, but dozens of times people came and tried to rescue us. Religious people, you know, because you were the tent show. There were a lot of people who tried to rescue us and save us." He talked about this without rancor or bitterness, but it must have been difficult for young boys to be confronted with meddling, even if well-meaning, people who basically told the boys by their words and actions that their parents were not raising them properly.[62]

Jack told of how the religious groups competed for them after their father died in 1945. The two boys were trying to finish high school but were virtually penniless since Art left them no inheritance and their mother was gone with her husband. He and Jean were going to two different Protestant churches in the town of Leuders, Texas. People from Jean's church tried to help him by buying him a suit of clothes; when the other church found out about that, some of the members decided to buy Jack a suit of clothes also, but he said he "didn't need a suit of clothes. What I really needed was food." He said that was about his low point regarding funds, and he resorted to hunting to supplement his diet. He said he and his brother never thought about asking for help because "we weren't proud; we were just individualistic. We never even thought about asking anybody for help. It was up to us to take care of it, so we took care of it."[63]

Thirty years after the end of Art Names's show, the twins readily talked about how their later lives were affected by their years traveling. Jean Names seemed to have the most negative memories and regretted that as a young person he was not a part of a community. In an extended discussion of the early days, he said that he had not thought about it so much before, but now he felt that "I just wasn't really so much a part of any society as now I would love to have felt that I was." He also wondered what the effect was on the young person's self-esteem. "I think it gives you probably an inflated sense of self-importance. You seem to be a separate kind of society." Of show business life he said, "I'm not sure it was very healthy, to tell you the truth."[64]

His twin brother seemed to believe the experience of those early years was more positive. "I think it had a more positive effect because I've got more gypsy in me," Jack said. "It made me realize that eventually I'd like to become more involved with mankind as a whole." He said he had never wanted to be tied down to one set way of life, and that probably came from his upbringing. "It certainly made you realize," he said, "that every person is an individual and you are ultimately alone. That did happen because you saw the transient quality of relationships, the transient quality of life." He really believed that he benefited in many ways because "the experience enabled us to cope with a lot of different things more easily."

Jack gave upbeat descriptions of his experiences. "I can remember those carefree days on the show. Those were really beautiful. The smell of canvas! God, every time I get near canvas that same smell comes back to me. All the beautiful times we had; they were really, really relaxing. It was pretty carefree." Jack mixed well and met new people easily. "It was really exciting to meet new people and to leave problems and other people behind. You'd leave your mistakes behind you and just move on," he said. "It kept you always excited, always on our toes, and living is really interesting moving around."[65]

Jean had some good memories as well. He felt one of the most important things he learned from his youth was acting, which improved his ability to be a good teacher. He said thirty years later, "The greatest acting jobs for me are right in front of my class. It's fantastic. Being an actor makes a good teacher. I do believe that."[66]

Both of the sons agreed that there was one detrimental impact on their later lives. Jean expressed the opinion that the traveling life made it difficult for him to form strong personal attachments and may have been responsible for his divorce in later life. He clearly had thought a great deal about this problem in the years after his father died and worried about the psychological impact the life had on him. Jack agreed that close personal relationships were hard to form and sustain with all the moving around they did. He recalled, "For several years there we moved, and I think I got the feeling that the only way to live was to move for a long time. I think that really affects one, you know, a child like that." He said he always felt different as a young person. "I felt when I was young like I was almost from a different planet because it was a different way of life." Jack said that "one of the hardest things I ever had to do was to settle down to one relationship and one place. It was scary for me to come and settle down." Jack also believed that the influence of their early lives probably had a lot to do with their divorces.[67]

The Whisenhunt children never were influenced by life on the road the ways the Names children were. Of course, this was not really a way of life for the Whisenhunts; since for them it lasted for only a few seasons, the traveling was mostly just exciting.

SIX

Character, Politics, and Poetry

ART NAMES WAS THE HEART OF HIS OPERATION. WITHOUT HIM, Art Names Shows (or whatever name it operated under) would never have existed. He was the driving spirit behind everything that happened on his show; he was manager, actor, playwright, crewman, and morale builder, especially during hard times. Everyone who knew him noted his upbeat personality, even in the face of severe hardship. His honesty and his desire to provide wholesome entertainment without real concern for profit made him popular in the small towns of Middle America. Even twenty-five to thirty years after his death, just about everyone who remembered him spoke fondly of him. One is naturally inclined to believe that his personality must have had negative characteristics, but they are hard to find.

Names's personality and character were what made him special. His former wife and sons always commented on how honest he was, how he would never cheat a person or take advantage of a situation where he could have made a profit legally but perhaps not ethically. His former wife remembered his disdain for profit a bit bitterly, for she believed that he was always willing to help people and to forgo income that would have been beneficial to his family. His son Jack agreed with his mother, but he took a slightly different attitude about it, saying, "He didn't like a lot of profit." He said his father was not seeking great financial success but only wanted to support his family, run his show, and live life his own way. The other twin, Jean, did say that in the last few months of his life, Art was concerned about his sons and their completion of high school studies. He seemed to imply that his father was anxious about their future and somewhat concerned that he might not have provided for them as he could have had he been in some other line of work.

One of the characteristics always mentioned about Names was his honesty. His son Jack said, "He was the most honest person I've ever known. He was so honest it was unbelievable." Milburn Stone remembered Names's honesty, especially when dealing with town people along their circuit. Names told Stone that nothing was more important to him and that honesty was more responsible for his success than his professional reputation. If he treated the local people with a lack of respect, which is what dishonesty really is, he would have no future in the small towns of the Great Plains. He was scrupulous, Stone said, to deal honestly and fairly with everyone he came into contact with, even to the point that he sometimes backed off and took a loss. Even if he were right, he would take a loss to keep his reputation intact.[1]

Despite his desire to get along, Names was never one to take abuse from anyone, including town people. When he felt he was being wronged he could respond quickly and forcefully to make his point. Kenneth Whisenhunt recalled a time when a local teenager tried to take advantage of Names. During saltwater taffy sales one evening, two coupons for the large teddy bears were presented from one carton of candy. Names was nonplussed, for he knew he had put only one coupon in the carton, but more than that, one of the coupons presented was not typed by Names. Clearly, the young man who presented the coupon had typed it himself on a typewriter with a font quite different from that on Names's machine. Names knew that if he made a public issue of a false coupon, the audience would think he was not honoring his word and was taking advantage of one of the town's teenagers. Therefore, Names gave away two teddy bears that night.

Names knew the boy who had presented the counterfeit coupon and was well acquainted with the family. The next day, Names went to see the boy's father and explained to him what had happened. He showed the father the difference between the typed coupons and explained what the boy had done. Names played it exactly right as he told the father he was not trying to get the teddy bear back, nor was he trying to get the boy in trouble. He had gone to the father because he thought the boy's parents should know about his dishonesty, as he, as a concerned parent himself, would want to be told if his own sons were doing something dishonest. It worked like a charm. The father confronted the son, and he admitted what he had done. The father required the boy to go to Names and apologize for his actions and return the bear. Names made his point and protected himself at the same time.[2]

In a letter to Names, Hazel B. Ross, the widow of his former partner, Joe Sims, praised Names for his honesty. She said, "Joe used to say you & he never 'checked short' even a 2 ct stamp."[3]

Names's honesty was reflected in a story told by Milburn Stone who remembered a time in the late 1930s when he was back in Kansas and had made a point to see Names. He said Art had owed him three hundred dollars for a few years. Art had never made any effort to send it to Stone, but Stone was confident that if he ever went to Art and asked for it, he would pay it even if he had to sell something to get the money. When Stone had been with Names for just a few minutes that day, Names "peeled off a roll of bills and paid me. Right to the penny."[4]

Stone also remembered when they were doing a show in a town in Kansas a man came looking for Names because the man's son had not received his pass to the show for helping erect the tent. Stone said the boy did not get the pass because he had not stood in line like the other boys. The father, angry when he came looking for Names, accosted Stone and asked, "Who is the head nigger?" He told Stone he had come to "whup up on somebody." The man was directed to Names and began to curse him. When the man would not listen to reason, Names slapped him with the flat of his hand on the chest and kept slapping him on the chest and backing him up inside the tent. He caught the man by surprise, not giving him a chance to relax. Finally he got the man to calm down, and they talked it out. Names violated his principles of nonviolence for his own protection, but he was not happy about it. Names told Stone, and others through the years, that he had seen so much fighting when he was a boy and in the war that he could not think of a reason he should engage in violence.[5]

Art's son Jack remembered years later that his father really cared about people; he "was always willing to talk . . . was happy to talk. Just really a stimulus to be around. He had stimulated people; he excited people. He seemed to love all of humanity." He said his father was not interested in promoting his vision or taking advantage of other people. "I think he was really interested in people and acting and plays and his way of life. You know, he wanted to be free."[6]

Other people remembered his interest in talking, whether on the stage, to other people, or to his sons. Whisenhunt's wife remembered that when his boys were teenagers and they misbehaved, Names had two ways of dealing with them. If he felt one of them needed some sort of punishment, he would give him a sledgehammer and a stake that was used to hold the tent in place. He would take the boy into a vacant lot and tell him to drive the stake into the ground, then pull it out, and then drive it into the ground again. He was to do this until he understood the importance of his misbehavior and resolved not to do it again.

Kenneth Whisenhunt remembered that sometimes Art would fine the boys

CHARACTER, POLITICS, POETRY

if they did something wrong. Jack agreed, "Yeah, right, he used to fine us. Another punishment he had for us was to have us stand on a block for a while as the others tore down the tent and loaded it for moving."[7]

On other occasions, he would take the son who had misbehaved and put him arm around the boy's shoulder. He would walk away with the boy talking intently into his ear. They might be gone two minutes or it might be ten minutes. No one except the two of them ever knew exactly what was said, but clearly Names was trying to talk the situation out with his son.[8]

Names's personal behavior was above reproach, as far as the record reveals. He told one of Whisenhunt's sons that he did not know whether he liked whiskey or not since he had never tasted it. He did say that he knew he did not like beer because he tasted it once and could not stand it.[9] Jack said that his father told him once that he never even had an urge to smoke or drink because he might be subject to addiction and did not want to take a chance. Names told his son, "I don't want to ever be exposed to them because I might develop a habit." This may well have been a reaction to his alcoholic father. Jack said, "That's the only time I've known his mind to be closed to anything. He was one of the few men I've ever known who never drank, never swore, never smoked."[10]

A man from the South Plains of Texas, Odell Hogan, remembered Names very well. He said that Art had picked him up in West Texas, and he worked for Art for about six years on two different occasions. He was convinced that Names saved him from getting into trouble. Hogan told the story of how, when Art was playing in the town of Lorenzo, Texas, a man came to Art and asked for work. Art told him he could not pay anything, but if the man wanted to work he would give the man a free pass all week for his whole family. It turned out the man had a wife and seven children. "We sure got a laugh on him about that, but to Art, he was most pleased, believe he would have felt better if he had had an even dozen. He was just that kind of man." The man with the large family lived in a building next to the lot where the tent was located. In front of the building he had a small fruit and vegetable stand, but with no produce. Since the show did well that week and Art had a little extra money, he loaned the man enough money to stock his stand with vegetables, asking only for some black-eyed peas and tomatoes. Hogan said that about a year later he was working for a competing stage show when it played in the neighboring town of Ralls. He decided to go to Lorenzo to see a girl he had met there the year before. When he got to town he went by the vegetable stand and was shocked to find that the man Art had helped had expanded his store and stocked it with groceries as well as fruits and vegetables. Hogan did not say if Names ever knew of the success of the man he had loaned money to, but even if he had, Names would never have taken credit for the success, for, as so many people said, "That's just the kind of man he was."[11]

There were many other testimonials to Names's character and behavior. Though he surely must have had faults that no one mentioned, it is clear that Art Names was a man people loved and respected.

Another feature of Names's personality was his upbeat attitude. At times, some town people questioned his sincerity since he seemed always to be happy and never seemed to "get the blues" or to "get down in the dumps." Most people have their bad times and days when they are not very pleasant, but Names seldom exhibited such behavior. Surely, Names had his negative characteristics, but no one who knew him would say anything negative about him thirty years later. He took a fairly philosophical attitude toward life's adversities. Stone said, "I used to say that if somebody went to Art and said your tent burned down, somebody killed your dog, and one of the twins is gone or died, Art would walk away whistling."[12] Names was well known for his whistling. Kenneth Whisenhunt recalled, "It seemed like the more trouble he had or more difficulties he ran into, the more he would whistle."[13]

Most people who remembered Names agreed that he was not religious in any formal sense. From day to day, he tried to live a moral life, but this was based more on the Golden Rule than any formal religious guidelines. His plays often had biblical references, sometimes quoted scripture, and occasionally had moralistic overtones. There is no evidence that these were particular views of Names; perhaps he wrote plays with these ideas to please his rural, conservative, Protestant audiences.

Most people agreed that Names believed in God but seldom went to church and never participated in organized religion.[14] Near the end of his life after the partnership with Whisenhunt ended, he was living in Leuders, Texas, with his son Jean and was trying to get the show going again. Jean became interested in religion and began attending church in the community, and his father would go with him occasionally. Jean said, "I knew at the time that he had really very little sympathy in that direction, but he went just to please me."[15] The other twin, Jack, agreed with his brother. He believed his father to be a moral person, but he was the kind of person who rejected organized religion and questioned the sincerity of publicly pious people.[16]

Perhaps Milburn Stone described Names's spiritual views most accurately: "I think that Art felt that every step he took in his life at that moment or any

CHARACTER, POLITICS, POETRY

other moment he was as close to God as anybody else in the world could possibly be. And that's the way he lived. I think he didn't feel he had to go to any medium or any structure to have a spiritual life." Still, Names never expressed any religious beliefs to Stone. Stone summed it up by saying, "All the religious beliefs I think that he expressed were philosophical beliefs. After all, what is religion if it's not a good philosophy?"[17]

Names's personal life was scarred by his divorce from Maurine. Few people would talk about—or actually knew—the reasons for the divorce. Maurine was the one who knew best, but she did not say much about what caused them to separate. The interesting feature of their divorce was the close relationship that continued between the two of them, even after Maurine's remarriage. The fact that Maurine and her new husband could come back to the rejuvenated repertoire show as actors and have a good relationship with Art speaks to strong characters of both Maurine and Art. Beulah Whisenhunt was always amused by the fact that long after they were divorced, Art went to Maurine's trailer house every morning when her husband was out of town and carried out her chamber pot. She would often call out the door of the trailer for Art, and he would come right away and run errands or do chores for her. Beulah often thought that Names acted more like a husband after they were divorced than before.[18]

Names never became involved with another woman after the divorce, according to his sons. Jack Names said his father never seemed to regret anything about his life, even the divorce. "It must have been pretty painful to him, and yet he never seemed to regret it, and he never became that interested in another woman again. He was interested in women, but never interested enough to marry again. He chose his way of life."[19] The other twin, Jean, agreed: "He didn't smoke, he didn't drink, and he didn't run around. That's when I knew him. Now Mother probably has a different story, but at least when he was with me, he didn't."[20]

Maurine did hint that Art had a roving eye, and there may have been instances during their marriage when there were other women in Art's life; she said she had a difficult life with Names.[21] There is little other evidence to support a claim that he was unfaithful. Art was an outgoing man who had many friends, both male and female. There were always town girls and young women who were attracted by the excitement of show business and who came around the tent when they could. Whether Art ever had any relationship with any of these women is not known.

After his divorce, and especially when he was alone and at his lowest point about 1940, he carried on an extensive correspondence with the widow and the daughter of his former partner, Joe Sims. The letters to Helen B. are warm and friendly, but those to the daughter, Betty Jo, who at that time was a senior in high school, suggest that Names had a more physical interest in the young girl. They can be interpreted as nothing more than letters of friendship and advice from an older person who might be playing the role of an uncle, but the language is more personal than one would expect in such correspondence. If Betty Jo reciprocated any personal feelings, there is no existing written evidence.[22]

Names clearly did not have much interest and little involvement with women in the last years of his life. Since life on the show was not very private, relationships could not be hidden very well, and involvement with other women apparently did not occur.

Clearly, Names was a complex man. He was more philosophical and intellectual than the stereotype of show business people would suggest. He had a strong interest in people and made friends everywhere he went, but, at the same time, he spent a good deal of time alone in introspection and had definite ideas about a wide range of subjects, with a strong interest in political matters. Some of the plays Names wrote in the 1910s and 1920s reflect his political views and deal with some of the social and political issues of the day, but the political content was usually played down since his primary goal was to entertain. When hard times came to America in the 1930s, Names began to think more specifically about the country's problems and, like many other Americans, to seek solutions for the ills besetting the country. Some of these views are reflected in the plays he wrote during the 1930s.

By the time of the divorce between Art and Maurine Names, Art began to think more specifically about going into politics directly. Records are very sparse, but based on family accounts and hints in the surviving papers of Names, one can conclude that after his wife left, Names used his time alone to refine his political views.

As he witnessed the suffering of Americans throughout the plains and as he suffered through the Dust Bowl days himself, he became more angry that such conditions could exist in a nation as rich as America. Through the late 1930s he paid attention to the events in Europe, especially the increasing threat to world peace exhibited by Hitler and Mussolini. Names could see the United States edging closer and closer to war and when fighting began in Europe in 1939, he was more convinced that the United States would get involved. He did not trust that the neutrality laws of the 1930s would protect the United States from the passions of war, and when Franklin Roosevelt openly expressed his concern for and support of Great Britain, Names became more discouraged.[23]

In 1940, Names spent much time in contemplation. He was able to keep his show running by showing motion pictures, but attendance was small and he never knew if he would be able to open the next day. Spending time alone caused him to be more introspective, and he became more concerned about politics. He was very anxious about the war that had begun in Europe in 1939 and whether the United States would get involved. He had also become disenchanted with America's political leadership and seemed, at times, to despair for the future.

The Great Depression may well have influenced Names's political views as much as anything else. He was clearly influenced by the antiwar sentiment of the 1930s. The hearing conducted by the Nye Committee on the causes of America's entrance into World War I concluded that American entry had been unduly influenced by bankers trying to protect their investments and the munitions makers who saw the opportunity for great profits.[24] When these revelations were made, the already isolationist sentiment of most Americans was enhanced. Names said in some of the random thoughts he wrote down that he had been born of middle-class parents who worked hard for what they had and though he would not have been disloyal to the United States for any reason, he still could be concerned about the direction the country took in World War I. In the aftermath of his own service, he was able to understand that the motives for entering may well not have been the pure altruistic goals for democracy that Woodrow Wilson had espoused.

After the invasion of Poland in 1939, Names wrote a document he titled, "We Are About to Engage in Another War to Make the World Safe for Democracy," a sarcastic title, but one which reflected his concern. He believed that America's leaders were not doing enough to keep the country out of war, but by this time, he had lost faith in almost all American leadership. The first paragraph of this document reflects his feelings as well as anything else: "We are now face to face with a world wide conflict which is bound to make the wars of the past seem puny and bloodless; if that war comes, you and I will be a part of it; its limits will be boundless and its horrors will be beyond description. Surely our preparation for that war is a worthy cause; and surely any honorable step to avoid that war is even still more worthy."[25]

Names's concern about government and war evolved into a general disenchantment with government. One document that can be dated to about 1935 reflects his changing philosophy. At that time he did not support the attacks on the munitions makers that were coming from the Nye Committee; he said, "Beware of the politician who has an axe to grind against ammunition makers and armament makers and accuses them of all manner of evil."[26] Names was not a pacifist even though he wanted America to stay out of war. He did not belong to the America First Committee or other extremist groups, but he was clearly skeptical of the government. He believed in defense and strength in peacetime—at least in 1935. By 1940 he still believed in national defense, but he was more inclined to support efforts to keep America out of the European war.

Considering Names's attitude about politicians in general, his comments about munitions makers are interesting. He believed in experts doing the jobs they were trained to do and used the analogy of doctors and mechanics doing their jobs and how foolish a person was who would not allow them to do the things they were trained for. "Only a fool will sneer at a doctor when he is healthy. Only a fool will shoot a good mechanic when his car is running smoothly. Only a fool will be a stumbling block in the way of a munitions maker when there is peace in the world." He asked if the average person could set broken bones or repair his own car and concluded, "If you can fight your own wars with your old shotguns then cremate your munitions makers."[27]

He became more disenchanted with political leaders every year. He reflected the "rugged individualism" that has been so much a part of American thought and did not support various movements during the 1930s that extended the role of government. His politics are not known, but coming as he did from Kansas, a traditionally staunch Republican state, one can assume that he was a Republican.

Names was particularly bothered by the "Share the Wealth" program promoted by Senator Huey Long of Louisiana and the movement for a government old-age pension program led by Dr. Francis Townsend. He saw these as unwarranted government intrusion and programs that would sap the strength of the country. Regarding the Long proposal, he said, "If labor and capital are fair with each other there will be no need to share the wealth because it will be possible for an honest man to make plenty. If they be not fair no amount of laws or share the wealth can equalize the burden."[28] In addition, he believed pension programs were an insult to the old because "we are mocking old age and making fools of ourselves" when we support old people. He asked how Americans could support the aged when they did not even support the young.

The problem in the 1930s, he said, was that Americans "are depending

CHARACTER, POLITICS, POETRY

upon leaders instead of ourselves,"[29] something that sapped strength and initiative and made the professional politicians too powerful. He was equally critical of Democrats and Republicans. Politicians, he thought, were the problem. The answer was simple: take government out of the hands of the professionals whose only concern was reelection and who swayed with the wind. As long as they were in control, the future would be bleak.

On one occasion, he wrote that what the country needed more than anything was economic freedom. This was so important that he felt the Constitution should be amended to separate political and economic life because political freedom could not exist without economic freedom. In the current situation political leaders controlled economic life, and the two things had to be separated. He said, "There will never be economic freedom as long as the politicians control our economic life. It is impossible to put politics and economics in the same bed."[30] Names never said exactly what changes had to be made in the Constitution to achieve his goals, but he continued to rail, at least in private, against politicians and to advocate "economic freedom."

Names very seldom dated anything and there is no way to know how representative the surviving material is of his thinking. By piecing together references to his age and other hints, the material available today appears to have been written between 1935 and 1940, mostly in 1938 and after. Much of what survives appears to be different versions of the same document.

In his writing, Names criticizes government without naming individuals. He attacks "politicians," saying that America's basic problem is that it has passed from the hands of statesmen to politicians. The "statesmen" that he most often mentions are George Washington, Abraham Lincoln, and Robert E. Lee. The inclusion of Lee into this list is interesting since he never held elective office and is not often considered a hero or "statesman" by Kansans and other midwesterners.

His heroes were people like Henry Ford, and Names liked comparing government to business—especially the automobile business. Ignoring his antilabor and anti-Semitic views, Names said that Henry Ford was the best example of the statesman in business. Solutions to current problems could be solved by "automobile sense," "using the same brain processes in government that we now use in the manufacture, buying and selling and repairing of automobiles."[31]

Names finally decided to do something about the problems he saw. He decided to run for office—to be governor of Kansas—a decision he apparently made in late 1938. He drafted numerous versions of an announcement of his candidacy; one of the more interesting ones explained that he would be "a candidate for the office of Governor of Kansas in 1940 (also I anticipate in 1942). In fact I am a candidate for the office of Governor of Kansas until I get elected, or shot, or in the course of time die a slow and natural death." The decision was not out of the blue, he suggested. "This feeling of mine THAT I SHOULD TAKE OFF A FEW MINUTES FROM MY DAILY TASKS AND ASSIST IN RENOVATING THE GOVERNMENT is not just a sudden inspiration on my part, or a rash decision at which I have only newly arrived, but it is the logical result of 47 years of patient waiting on my part for somebody else to do the things which we have long known SHOULD BE DONE and which we all realize eventually MUST BE DONE."

Despite his dramatic statements, the surviving material shows him to be quite vague on specifics. In the Names material is one copy of a mimeographed newsletter called *Art Names Weekly* that was "edited by Art Names of the Kansas Authors Club." Nothing more is known about this publication—how long it lasted, whether it was distributed widely, and the dates it might have published. He called himself a "political mechanic" who was not a politician and who would not be influenced by the usual political considerations.

Names constantly used the word "coordination" as the major plank in his platform without much explanation. His writing reflects quite a naive view of government, and he never gets down to specifics, but he continually rails against the politicians and calls up the images of Washington, Lincoln, and Lee. "My country needs a Washington. But there still is no Washington! And so I shall be WASHINGTON! And why not? Am I not a man? (of a sort) And after all, Washington was only a man (But what a man!)"[32]

Names constantly referred to himself as a fool and sometimes called himself "a fat fool." In fact, he uses the word "fool" often throughout his political writing and occasionally in his poetry; in the scripts of his plays, he often uses the expression "we who are fools." In one of his statements of principle, he said:

I am indeed only a fool and my only virtue is that I am not in the least afraid to rush madly in where angels fear to tread. And now that I know the truth about the condition of our glorious government, I am not afraid to try to save it.

Now that my decision is made, it cannot be changed. I shall at once proceed to joust flopping windmills across the wide expanse of our

CHARACTER, POLITICS, POETRY

land. Feeble fool which you find me here at the beginning, you will find me that same inspired idiot on the last page of the last chapter. I shall at least be consistant [*sic*], even though that may well be my only virtue....

I am only a FOOL—I can never be a Washington or Lincoln or a LEE, but I still have this in common with that mighty trio—I am not afraid to try and I am not afraid to die.[33]

The seriousness of Names's candidacy cannot be determined. Various state officials in Kansas who examined the election records can find no evidence that he ever filed for office or that he received any votes.[34] He published his *Art Names Weekly* at least once, and he regularly listed himself as a candidate for governor of Kansas in show-business advertising in 1939 and 1940. As mentioned earlier, he talked about it enough that family and friends thought he was actually a candidate. During 1940 he was not in Kansas much of the time, but that did not disqualify him since he always maintained his official residence in McCracken, Kansas, at least until he became a partner with Whisenhunt.

During the early part of 1940, the subject of several of his letters to Helen B. Ross Sims and her daughter, Betty Jo, was his gubernatorial candidacy. During 1940—probably in February, based on inference from the letter—he wrote to Betty Jo from Ropesville, Texas, about the "their plan." He said that a snowstorm had blown in, a storm serious enough that the city of Lubbock was closed in. He says they (he and Betty Jo) are partners in this venture, but the letters are not clear what he means by "partner." He told Betty Jo that Art, Jr., who was with him at this time, thought their plan was a "knockout" and was helping Art with it. "But," Art commented rather sadly, "it is having a hard time surviving—Everytime we get ready to spring it on the Public, we have a storm—"[35] One could infer from this that as of February, 1940, he had not made a public announcement of his candidacy. But that does not square with two advertising brochures that announce two plays featuring Jack and Ilaferne Campbell, his partner from 1939 and his wife. These brochures are undated but clearly predate his letter to Betty Jo from Ropesville since by that time (February, 1940), the Campbell partnership was no more.[36]

He wrote several times to Betty Jo and her mother about the project, always alluding to the "Enterprise" or the "Infant Industry" or their "project." He never openly says that he is talking about his candidacy.[37] In another letter to Betty, he says that he had a letter from her mother and she wanted to in-

TENT SHOW

vest "two or three cents in it." He also explained that Art, Jr., wanted to join as some kind of partner—"not sure what kind"—but he and Art, Jr., had performed a "concert" the night before and billed it as a "benefit" performance for the "venture." They brought in $4.15 from the "concert." This would suggest that he was telling people that he was a candidate, but in his letters he continues to use euphemisms to describe it. He concluded in this letter, "We have a right popular organization it seems—(but don't know for how long—till we go broke I guess)."[38]

Whether he was serious in his candidacy is difficult to determine. He was out of the state most of the year, he never filed for office, and he never campaigned in a formal sense. One might argue that he used this as an advertising gimmick that might improve his business if the public thought he was some kind of celebrity. The surviving material clearly shows that he was concerned about government, but there is little evidence to prove that his candidacy was serious, despite the belief of his family and friends that it was.

In addition to Names's concern about government and public affairs, he also had a literary side. Names had a reputation as a poet among his contemporaries. How prolific a poet Names was is impossible to determine since there is no way to know how much the small collection of surviving poems reflects his lifetime production. On first glance, there appear to be about twenty surviving poems, but on closer examination, one can see that various versions of the same poem exist, and he sometimes moved verses around from one poem to another. Probably there are fourteen original separate pieces, not a very large body of work, but they may be only a small portion of his compositions.

The surviving poems, in most cases, are difficult to date. Some do not even have titles and are merely verses that may be complete, may have been works in progress never completed, or may have been included in longer versions that are now lost. The earliest poem that can be dated is from 1911, and the latest is a poem about World War II and Art Names, Jr.'s role in it, published and copyrighted in pamphlet form in 1944 by Jack and Jean Names. Some of his poems clearly were written in the 1930s because they reflect the struggle that Names was having during the Great Depression.

The earliest poem is an untitled one that Names sent to his friend Lida Floyd in McCracken, Kansas, written on the letterhead of a law firm in Lyons, Kansas. This was the time when Names was attempting to go to law school, and he may have been clerking in this firm or "reading law." The poem is humorous and not very "good" poetry since it is simplistic and concentrates

CHARACTER, POLITICS, POETRY

on rhyme. At the time Names was about twenty-two years old. He mentions in the poem that he is writing plays as well as poetry, showing clearly that he was still interested in the theater, even though he probably was studying law at the same time. The poem reflects the early work of Names.

> **Dear Friend Lida:**
> **Down to my typewriter I'll sit**
> **and try to rhyme a little bit.**
> **The meter may not be first rate**
> **and all the feet may not be straight,**
> **But still I hope in it you'll find some little good.**
> **Be not unkind For if you don't say this is fine,**
> **I'll never write another line.**
> **We had a little rain last night**
> **but now the sun is shining bright;**
> **The day is just like one in summer,**
> **I'll tell you what it is a hummer.**
> **Tell Florence, Bob and Ruth Hello**
> **and all the other folks I know.**
> **My drama's done and I will state**
> **that I do think it is first rate,**
> **The other folks of course, you see,**
> **may think it punk as punk can be.**
> **When I get stamps enough ahead,**
> **I'll send it to you as I said.**
> **This poetry is pretty bad**
> **and so to stop I better had.**
> **Hoping to hear from you, I now**
> **will sign my name and make my bow.**
>   **Arthur Names**[39]

About a month later Names sent another poem to the same person that shows a more serious side. Like many poets he asks what life is all about.

> **"Come drink with us now**
>   **And drown all your sorrow,**
> **For tonight you will die**

> And there's nothing
> tomorrow"
> Some call that life,
> But, if they are right,
> I do not care
> To go on with the fight.

Names follows with his own conclusions.

> We do have our moments
> Of sorrow and woe,
> But we too have our hours
> Of the bright sunlight's glow,
> And our moments of darkness
> But help us to see
> All the better the joys
> Of life's sunlit sea.
> If I did not think
> That this was the way
> I would not go on
> With the struggle to day.[40]

The next poem that can be dated was written on December 17, 1917, from Camp Lewis, Washington, where Names was serving in the Medical Detachment, 316th Engineers. This poem, also to Lida Floyd, is humorous and reflects the attitudes of many people toward the Pacific Northwest:

> Dear Friend Lida:
> drop,
> drop,
> drop!
> Will this raining never stop?
> Everywhere the rain is dripping,
> dripping, dripping,
> down
> on me—
> When they blow Taps in the ev'ning and at morning reveille;

drip,
  drip,
 drip!
Everywhere you go you slip!
And you stumble over pebbles which were once the Ocean bed
And you fall into a mud hole where the little Salmon fed.
  shine,
    shine,
  shine!
Shine your shoes and get in line,
Never mind the rainy weather, it will clear up by and by—
We'll be leaving O'er the spring time and the rain stops in July

  glances,
    glances,
      glances,

He concludes the poem:

Back to dear old Kansas—
  If I ever do get back,
  You can bet your bloomin' "jack"
I'll just sit and watch the sunshine coming down across the plain
And though it's as dry as blazes I will never yell for rain.
    Your friend,
    Names

At the bottom of the page, he wrote,

    "Jan. 2, 1917 [he probably meant 1918]
    It's still raining.
    n.[41]

Names's best poem from a literary perspective was a five-verse poem he titled "The Purple Sea," which discusses Kansas in prehistoric days, evokes several images, and is a good tribute to the state. Dating the poem is difficult. Zippa Hall, who said that she knew Names when she was teaching school in Ness City, Kansas, and often went to McCracken for the weekend, said about

"The Purple Sea," "I have always been impressed with this poem—and have kept it in a scrap book." She had always thought it ranked with "Call of Kansas" by Esther Clark, which had been used as a state poem. She said, "I have often thought this should be used as a state poem—as Esther Clark's has been."[42] It reads, in its entirety:

> This was the bed of the foaming sea
> Whereon I stand today
> And the wind which tosses this gnarled tree
> And whips these dusty weeds at me
> Once mingled the ocean spray.
>
> But that ocean which used to be is dead
> At rest in the ground it lies
> And where a slimy monster sped
> A tumbleweed tosses its tousled head.
> Across the main it flies.
>
> Man tills the soil where the shellfish lie
> Asleep in their limestone graves
> And the ocean which rises to meet the sky
> Where once the salty brine flew high
> In an ocean of purple waves.
>
> And where of old the seagulls flew
> And dove to their final doom
> A sunflower tosses the long days thru
> And the honeybee sips of the fragrant dew
> As he dives in the purple bloom.
>
> Where once the ocean waves rolled free
> Now rolls the purple sod
> And the breezes which tossed that ancient sea
> Now carry a sweet perfume
> Like a breath from the lips of God.[43]

Another poem, probably written during the Great Depression, was humorous but dealt with the hard facts of the times. This poem reflected the Names

CHARACTER, POLITICS, POETRY

attitude that surfaces in other places—that of acceptance of what life has to offer:

There's times when you "work and win"
There's times when you "can't quite make it"
   There's times you can't fight
   Cause you can't tell what's right
So you grin and stand pat and take it!

There's times when you cuss and swear
   There's times when you sing and laugh—
      Then you hold to your breath,
      Cause you're scared half to death
As you grin and take the gaff.[44]

Another untitled poem pokes fun at the tattered condition of his tent and shows the difficulty Names was having during the Depression:

"It can't be much
Or it wouldn't be such
   A dump." and he laughed as he said it
He looked at the sign
And the name there was mine
   And he roared again as he read it

"Art Names show"
"Well, it better not blow
Or the derned thing will go into space
   It's raveled and worn,
   Its [sic] tattered and torn
What holds the derned thing in it's [sic] place?"

Well boys, I lowed,
   I'm jist mighty proud
Of that old rag you're making fun of
That funny old rag that I love!
   And cursed her
   And nursed her

Through all of her pains
I've stitched her
And pitched her
All over the plains

I've stayed up all night
And guyed her out tight
I've helped with her struggles and strains
She's a mighty good tent
And I love every rent
And she only leaks, gents, when she rains[45]

Another untitled poem shows Names's philosophical attitude toward life. Four verses compare life to the times a suit can be worn, the times an engine will run, the number of grains in the sea, and the number of times the Earth will turn. Then he concludes:

Life is at best but a shooting star
And the end is near or the end is far
But the end will come to me
And when it does I wont be short
I'll stand my ground and hold the fort
And play my last card like the kind of sport
I want my sons to be![46]

Names always thought of himself as a common man who sought no fame or great riches and wanted to live his life as he wished without interference. He was not common in some ways, but his identification with this type of person probably made it possible for him to succeed as long as he did. One of his poems, "The Common Cuss," talks about how the "common cuss" just tried to get by even though he was not accepted by most of society. The concluding two verses sum up his attitude about such people:

He didn't try to carve a name
Into the granite rock of fame
But he was contented to grind along
And toil and sing his little song.

CHARACTER, POLITICS, POETRY

And I'm glad that in all of this strife and fuss
I happened to know that common cuss.

So here's to the health of the common cuss,
And here's to the health of the rest of us
    For, when we die—and die we must,
    And all return to that common dust,
And get to the end of this mortal muss,
We'll go to sleep with the common cuss.[47]

One of the surviving poems about the death and burial of an unborn child
is difficult to interpret. Why Names wrote this is unclear, since there is no
evidence that his wife had a miscarriage or a stillbirth. That may have happened, but none of the family ever mentioned it. This is the most emotional
poem among the surviving poems, as the last verse shows:

Last night I laid my dreams away
    (and said a silent prayer!)
And there was no one near
                    to hear
    (and only me to care!)
An ageless longing in my breast
I softly laid away to rest;
A little baby, still unborn,
Lay in the dewy arms of morn
I touched his lips and smiling brow
I laid him softly in the grave
    (Because I loved him so!)[48]

There is a lengthy poem in the collection that reflects another facet of
Names's philosophy. The poem is untitled, but the extensive use of the phrase
"Am I Immortal?" suggests that may have been its title. Nowhere else in anything Names wrote is there any indication that he may have believed in reincarnation, but in this poem, there is the hint of it. One verse shows this
possible interpretation:

Today I am a lump of clay,
Tomorrow I shall rot away;

> The refuse 'neath the feet of men
> But I shall spring to life again!
> And you shall breathe me in the air
> And you shall find me everywhere!
> You plant me vainly in the sod—
> For always I shall rise again—A GOD![49]

Most likely, however, he was not talking about reincarnation but about the self as a symbol of all life:

> AM I IMMORTAL?
>   Answer this—
> When Earth was by the first Sun kissed
> And Dawn's first breath swept Earth's first mist
> And Time was caught by Earth's first breeze
> And lulled to sleep on Earth's first seas,
> WAS NOT I THERE?
>
> No LIFE was there—but I was there,
> An ATOM floating in the air![50]

Most of Names's poems were not deeply philosophical, but he did often deal with serious subjects. Some of the poems were comments on the times, especially the Depression and World War II, but his sons were important subjects as well. A number of surviving poems are about the Names sons or are advice he wrote to them. They were most likely written in the late 1920s or the 1930s as the boys grew into adolescence. In one he tells the boys that wanting to be rich and famous is a laudable aim but that they should be prepared for what might happen. His concluding verse says it best:

> If you want to be happy whoever you are,
> That must be your one—your guiding star—
> STAND RIGHT UP AND LAUGH AT YOU, WITH 'EM![51]

Some of the poems clearly were written when the boys were small, possibly to encourage them when they were living with the Dethricks in Oklahoma.

One poem that appears in several versions under more than one title deals with the world he lived in and what the older generation was leaving to the

CHARACTER, POLITICS, POETRY

next generation. There are several versions called "To Our Sons!" and another version titled "We, Who Dream." After World War II began, he rewrote and expanded the poem, titling it "To My Favorite Soldier." Jack and Jean Names published this version in 1944. The poet had hoped to leave his sons a world of peace, but the dreams and idealism of an earlier age had turned to dust. Several of the verses are somewhat pessimistic:

> But, as I view what I leave you,
> Here I stand—ASHAMED! DISMAYED!
> And may YOU and GOD forgive me
> For the blunders I have made!
>
> There's a dearth of laughing children,
> Where sweet laughter ought to ring!
> There's a wealth of weeds and wishes,
> Where the Seeds of Joy should spring!
>
> There's a mass of plodding people,
> Where no people ought to plod!
> There's a heap of pain and sickness
> In these Images of God!
>
> There's a struggle for existence,
> Where no struggle ought to be!
> There's a lot of plain injustice
> In this Kingdom of the Free!
>
> GRAFT and GREED! FILTH and CORRUPTION!
> And a BATTLE'S BELCHING GUN!
> In a WORLD, gone mad with war-lust!
> That is what I leave you, Son![52]

He then goes on to say that life is a struggle and people have to fight for what they want and what is right. People can dream for peace and justice, if they like, but not without strength and vigilance. He suggests that the pacifists are wrong. Some versions of the poem were written after the Japanese attack on Pearl Harbor, and Names reflects anti-Japanese sentiment in two of the verses:

Yet, we FOOLS, life's facts ignoring,
   Did with gentle phrases speak
And we said, "The STRONG shall tremble,
   As they stand before the MEEK!"
(When the HEATHEN HIT HAWAII,
   Did we stop them with our cheek?)

How we scoffed at heroes dying!
   How we sneered at fighting men!
Beat our shining swords to plough shares!
   Swapped our cannon for a pen!
(When Mikado bombed Manila,
   Did we stop him with that pen?)[53]

He makes another reference in some versions to the Japanese invading the United States, saying that the time for pacifism has ended and America must be defended at all costs:

You may sneer at heroes dying,
   You may scoff at daring men—
When the heathen knock at 'Frisco,
   Will you stop them with your pen?

He, who wants, has ever taken—
   He, who has, must still defend,
That was so in the beginning,
   It will be so 'til the end![54]

Names had served in World War I but had been disillusioned in the postwar era. Now war had come again and his oldest son was in the midst of it. He suggests in this poem that his generation had failed to protect the peace and now it was time for the next generation to do the job.

The most unusual poem that has survived is an extremely long composition entitled "Liberty." In typed form it runs more than twenty pages, more than a thousand lines, and is the most nontraditional of his work. This poem rhymes, but the lines and verses are not in traditional poetic form. The narrator of the poem goes back through history describing wars and efforts to obtain liberty without success. The narrator says that he was a lowly serf in

CHARACTER, POLITICS, POETRY

the Euphrates valley at the dawn of civilization and then becomes important people throughout history, ending with famous Americans such as George Washington and Abraham Lincoln. Essentially, this poem reflects the political views that Names was writing about in his so-called political campaign. In it he attacks politicians and blames them for the world's problems. A return to the leadership of statesmen is all that is needed, but, as in the political writing, there is little of substance to explain how this return to statesmanship can be achieved.[55]

Since Names's family kept a large quantity of his papers after his death, one could conclude that the surviving poetry is the bulk of what he wrote. Yet titles of Names plays have been identified for which no scripts can be found.

Clearly, Names was not an average man of his time. He had a strong character that was seen by almost everyone who knew him and he had strong views on public affairs. His chances in the electoral arena probably would have been nil, but at least he was concerned enough to consider alternatives and solutions. He had a creative streak that led him to write poetry, even if it might not be judged of very good literary quality. Again, like his political scribbling, his poetry reflected a contemplative side and a man who had strong ideas about the world in which he lived. These views were expressed as well in the plays that he wrote.

SEVEN

People's Playwright

JUST AS ART NAMES WROTE POETRY FOR HIS OWN GRATIFICATION and occasionally to recite to his audiences before performances, so too did he write original stage plays for his company to perform. Some might question the literary quality of his plays, but one must also consider that what entertains audiences has changed over the years and that his work was perfectly suited to his rural audiences.

There is a much larger body of surviving play scripts by Names than of poems. As with his poetry and political writings, there is no way to know how representative the surviving scripts are of his larger work, but, fortunately, enough scripts survive to give one a sense of his concerns and philosophy.

Like many, if not most, tent-show operators, Names wrote most of his plays to avoid paying royalty. Milburn Stone said that Names was always concerned about cost, and paying royalties was something that could easily be avoided. Stone said, "You did everything in the world to hold down the cost."[1] But there were other reasons that he wrote his own plays. He—and probably other tent operators—wrote his own plays because he could fashion them to fit his casts, especially during hard times when his company was greatly reduced from its earlier glory. With a smaller company to work with, he could rewrite his own plays to adjust them to smaller casts. In the early days he and his small company would move into indoor theaters during the winter. Since community opera houses or the high school auditoriums he used often were limited in stage equipment, the rewriting of scripts made it possible to adapt to these different conditions.[2]

On several occasions Names wrote a new play—or rewrote an earlier one—for a specific actor. Odell Hogan was a good example. Hogan said he worked for Names on two occasions—the first time Names "picked me up in West Texas about 1932 or 33, where I worked on Ranches & Farms. No edication [sic] & he was a second father to me . . . I am sure the route I was heading—I would no doubt have wound up in the pen, or jail."[3] Hogan said that Names wrote a play especially for him in which he played a bashful cowboy from Texas who was on the run in Kansas. Names staged the play under three different titles at different times: "The Texan," "The Stranger from Texas," and "The Stranger." Names, Hogan said, "always told me while he was writing the play, he would think of me just as I was, just an awkward bashful boy, using bad grammar & naturally had the Texas drawl."[4] Likewise, Geraldine Bradley Schultz said that Names occasionally wrote plays especially for her husband, Bernard "Bunny" Schultz, who played leads and Toby parts on the Art Names Show.[5]

Sometimes Names wrote new plays that related to current events, such as *Are You a Monkey?*, one of his most famous plays, written the same year as the Scopes "Monkey Trial" in Tennessee in 1925. Also during the 1920s he tried to capitalize on the nudism fad by writing a play about nudists. As World War II approached and the world was threatened by the rise of fascism, Names wrote several plays about the threat to peace and the rise of dictators. One of his last plays, for which no script can be found, was his own version of the story of the famous outlaw Jesse James.

Some rep owners wrote their own versions of stage plays of famous books or classics, but whether Names did this is not clear. A script for a play called *Rebecca of Sunnybrook Farm* is in the Names papers, but it does not appear to have been one written by him. It may well have been someone else's work that Names borrowed and produced or just had a copy of.

Piracy was common in the rep business since some rep owners were unscrupulous enough to steal the works of others. In the Names papers are three plays that had the notation on the scripts that they were the property of the Neal Stock Company or Henry Neal, a friend of Names, but no evidence exists that he used any of Neal's plays without his permission. Two other plays in his material do not appear to be his work. Besides *Rebecca of Sunnybrook Farm*, there was *The White Squaw*, a historical play set in the frontier community of Detroit in 1620. If this is a Names play, it is quite different from his other work and would represent a significant departure for him. More than likely this is a script that he acquired. Whether he ever produced it cannot be determined.

Generally speaking, there is no evidence that Names ever pirated plays of other people. He may have used the Neal plays sometimes, but if he did it was probably with the permission of Henry Neal. Milburn Stone was adamant that

Names would not pirate a play: "Art wouldn't do a thing like that. He would *never* do anything like that. He wouldn't steal from anybody."[6]

Because piracy was so easy, many playwrights, including Names, typed the parts for each character separately to make it more difficult to steal the play. Each actor had only his part with cues, often referred to as "sides," but not a copy of the entire play. Since photocopying was not yet available and much time and energy were required to type full scripts, playwrights found it much easier to produce "sides" for each actor, which also helped protect the playwright from having his play pirated.[7]

When Names was a partner with Joe Sims in the early 1920s, they collaborated on a few occasions in writing plays. But only two plays can be found with definite evidence of being cowritten by Names and Sims: *Home Brew*, written in 1921, and *Death Valley*, written in 1922.

Based on the Names papers, interviews with family and friends, and correspondence with people who knew him, a list of eighty-one plays that Names wrote was compiled. After adjusting for duplication, since several of the plays were produced under two or three different names, the list included seventy-six different plays. The memory of many people must be accepted since no scripts of some plays have survived. The sources seem fairly reliable as many of the titles for which there are no scripts were mentioned by more than one source.

A total of nineteen scripts that were very likely written by Names have been located. Copies of these scripts came from the Names papers, the Copyright Office of the Library of Congress, and Carolyn Thompson of McCracken, Kansas. Names was fairly diligent in his early years in copyrighting his plays, but in later years he did not do so as often.

In the Names papers, in addition to the full-length play scripts, were scripts for sixteen short pieces, some one- or two-page scripts for vaudeville-type bits that Names used for between-acts entertainment. These short scripts are not very original and may well be knockoffs of standard vaudeville bits that were performed by many companies. Some of them are corny and by today's standards seem juvenile; many of them were typical vaudeville blackouts, a widely used technique where a short sketch or comic bit builds to end in a blackout on the punch line or the curtain line. According to Don B. Wilmeth, "It can also mean a surprise ending to a scene or act with the lights going out quickly or a fast curtain."[8]

Of the seventy-six plays identified as being written by Names, only twenty-eight can be dated. Some of these dates are merely educated guesses, but others are based on the dates they were copyrighted or other notations on the scripts. Of the twenty-eight scripts that can be dated, three appear in 1912. Only one of those three survives; the other two are mentioned in news reports as being performed in McCracken or nearby communities. The last one that can definitely be dated is in 1941. If one assumes that Names wrote his first play(s) in 1912 and the last one *(Jesse James)* in 1944, then the seventy-six plays were written over a thirty-two year period and average about 2.3 per year. That would be in line with his wife's comments about his writing, "He set out when he got out of school to write two or three, at least, a year." She said when they went into theaters or during hard times, Names was not able to write much. "Whenever he'd start writing, he had to let everything else go. And whenever you start letting everything else go and let somebody else carry the load, well it [business] suffers."[9]

Names apparently liked to think he could write very fast, and Maurine confirmed that he could do so under trying circumstances. She told the story of how *Are You a Monkey?* was begun. They were visiting the parents of one of the men on the show who lived in Bucklin, Kansas, and "as we were all sitting around in the front room shooting the breeze and listening to each other and somebody else was at the piano and Art was sitting there with a pencil and he wrote part of *Are You a Monkey?*"[10]

On the written scripts for three of Names's plays he made a notation of when they were written and how long it took. On *A Lady in Distress*, he says, "First act written Aug 24 1927; second act Aug 26 1927; third act Aug 27 1927—All at Whitewater Kansas." On the title page of *The Game* he wrote, "Started at five p. m. Jan 4 1929 Finished 4:30 p. m. Jan 5 1929." For *The Return of the Devil* he noted, "This play written by Arthur A Names, of the Kansas Authors Club for presentation by his own dramatic company, Season of 1934. Time of writing—parts of three days—Place of writing—Afton, Texas."[11] These notations may have been only for his own information, but they seem to indicate as well that he wanted people to know he could write quickly.

The plays written by Names are typical of rep shows of his type. Most of them have rural themes and values that would appeal to rural audiences, and many are quite melodramatic. Even those that are serious in nature usually have a comic-relief feature—usually a Toby or a G-String character, who is such a country hick as to be almost unbelievable. In some of the plays there are serious problems of consistency or logic in the plots; audiences apparently were expected to suspend disbelief. Names's plays have a number of stereotypes that were common at the time, for blacks, Japanese, and Mexicans or Mexican Americans.

A number of the plays are clearly based on Names's life or, at least, take poetic license with things that happened to him or were familiar to him. For example, he wrote several plays that include twin children, though not always both boys as his were. Often the characters have the same names as members of his family, especially the twins, Jack and Jean, and his wife, whose name was spelled as both Maurine and Maureen.

It is clear that Names wrote plays that dealt, in one way or another, with issues of the time. Following the plays chronologically as much as possible, given that many of the plays are undated, the reader can see something of the evolution of Names's thinking.

The earliest play that can be dated is *Tyranny of Gold*. Names was only twenty-one years old when it was copyrighted in 1912, but it reflects some serious thinking about predestination, labor issues, poverty, poor girls going into prostitution, the insensitivity and cruelty of the rich, greedy doctors, corrupt politicians, and grasping businessmen with no concern about workers or the public. The meaning of the play's dedication to "The Great Unknown" is not clear, but it does make the play a bit mysterious. The play was well received when it was first presented in McCracken and neighboring communities.

The plot is rather convoluted, typical of several of the Names plays. By today's standards the play seems naive, though it does deal with some interesting issues. The discussion of predestination does not seem to be religion-based but is a prominent part of the plot. One character rails against it, saying, perhaps as Names felt: "Within each man who is a man is something that rebels at the thought that he is not his own master."

A part of the play deals with labor problems and the issues of wages and poverty. The businessman says, "When a man's out for the cash it isn't customary for him to have a conscience . . . If we can get a girl to work for us on starvation wages and the community will stand for it why that's the way we will do." One of the factory girls tells him that the workers cannot live decently on their wages, but the businessman responds, "You know how to earn extra if you dont." The girl responds heatedly, "Mr. Bensen, a poor girl cares for her virtue just the same as a rich one does. Would you want your daughter to earn money that way?" Bensen's response is pretty harsh: "You belong to a different class. If the poor people wasn't placed here to serve the rich, what the devil were they placed here for." Later in the conversation, he says, "Be thankful that we let you live," and still later, "Poor people are too particular." There is also criticism of doctors and their greed when a worker in the play says in his broken English, "Chee, dem doctor guys am expensive. Dere all out on de git rich scheme."

The class consciousness of the play is summed up in a fairly long speech of the lead character:

> **Your question is easily answered. We boast of a free government, of a free people and a free mind; we look at the political servitude of Russia and point with pride to our own republic; we hear the clank of chains in the far east and turn to our own slaves now free; we read of the Harems of Turkey and look with pride upon our own pure American womanhood. This being true, will we as American Citizens, consent for a moment that our daughters should work under conditions which appeal only to their baser passions? While the wealthy ride in their gilded cars of ease will we allow the flower of our American Womanhood to garnish the gutters? Will we demand that they work for wages that allow but the bare necessities of life?**

This play seems to reflect the concerns of Progressive reformers in the early part of the century; one of their major issues was the condition of women in the workplace.[12]

Another issue of the time that divided America as nothing else has was Prohibition. No script for one of Names's early plays from 1917, *Bone Dry*, has been found, but one can surmise from the title that it had to do with Prohibition. Another play that did survive from 1921, *Home Brew*, deals with Prohibition after it became law in 1920. Names coauthored this play with Joe Sims, his partner at the time who had a serious drinking problem.

The plot is somewhat confusing. It involves efforts to make beer, which is against the law, and the loss and recovery of the recipe. There are two detectives who are portrayed as such buffoons as to be totally unbelievable. As with many of Names's plays, there is misdirection, naïveté, and mistaken identities.

This play includes a number of racial and ethnic stereotypes. A Japanese character is upset that people think he is Chinese and should do the laundry, which he refuses because it is beneath him and only "Chinks" do laundry. There are some references to "Japs," the Empire of Japan, and the possibility of war with that country, an interesting reference made in 1921 when tension between Japan and the United States was minimal. There are several stereotypical references to Irish people as excessive drinkers, police officers, and Catholics. This is obviously a topical play dealing with a contemporary issue, but it is a farce and not serious in its dealing with the issue of Prohibition, on which it takes no stand.[13]

As mentioned earlier, Names also wrote about the controversy over evolution that became a national issue in the 1920s. *Are You a Monkey?* is probably his best-known and most successful play. It was written in 1925, the same year as the trial about the teaching of evolution in Dayton, Tennessee. A young teacher in Dayton, John Scopes, agreed to violate a Tennessee law about teaching evolution to test the validity of the law. Two leading men of the day, Clarence Darrow and William Jennings Bryan, went to Dayton to serve as opposing attorneys, and H. L. Mencken, the celebrated newspaperman from Baltimore, covered the case for his paper and made it a national event. Names decided to take advantage of the publicity by writing a comedy that would deal with this issue.

The play went through many versions. There is some suggestion that it may have actually been a five-act play in the beginning, but the version that was copyrighted in 1926 was four acts. Names presented this play many times over the years, sometimes in a shorter version for indoor theaters such as school auditoriums, where occasionally he used high school students as actors. One undated advertising flyer survives that advertises the play in the Meadow Grade School auditorium with high school actors.

The plots of the three-act and four-act versions are essentially the same. Both deal with a serum, invented by a doctor who has spent twenty-five years in Africa studying chimpanzees, that will turn a man into a monkey. The major plot deals with the doctor's effort to find someone on whom to test the serum. Subplots include romantic relationships among several characters and the anguish a minister feels as he changes from an opponent to a supporter of evolution. There is a "beast," but in one version he is a man who has been unfairly sent to a mental institution and in the other version he is a more ambiguous character who may actually be a cross between a man and a monkey. In one version the beast dies. The four-act version has an additional role, a female who adds a bit of mystery and possibly some sex appeal. She is a third female character, and Names, who was always short of women performers, must have cut this character from later versions to accommodate his company.

As in the case of Prohibition, Names tries to capitalize on a hot topic through comedy without taking a definite position on the issue itself. Still, his belief in evolution is implicit in the play. One might interpret this play as anti-religious, although he does not go that far in the dialogue or characters. It must have been risky for him even to broach this subject, given the audiences that he played to in Kansas in the 1920s.

The minister in the play does take a stand on evolution. At the beginning he preaches a sermon against it, but before the play is over he modifies his views, which he explains in a long speech:

> **Only yesterday that question also appeared very important to me, Doctor Surcey, but to-day I am seeing life in a different light. Of what importance is it to me if God created me from the virgin earth or if he descended me from an animal, if in either case he gave unto me the soul of a GOD? I can see the hand of God in the Jellyfish and in the rose. And to conceive of them as coming from a common life germ with myself suddenly becomes a beautiful thought. HE LIVETH BEST WHO LOVETH BEST ALL THINGS BOTH GREAT AND SMALL FOR THE DEAR GOD WHO LOVETH US—HE MADE AND LOVETH ALL![14]**

Another topical Names play had three different names, *A Lady in Distress*, copyrighted in 1927; *Two Black Crows*, copyrighted in 1928; and *Amos and Andy*, copyrighted in 1930. The first version, *A Lady in Distress*, is the one that Names noted was written in four days between August 24 and 27, 1927, in Whitewater, Kansas. The cast list in 1927 includes Milburn Stone; his wife, Loraine Smith; and Jack and Ilaferne Campbell. The third version in 1930 was named *Amos and Andy*, the same as the radio show that went nationwide in 1929 and became one of the most popular programs of all times. Names obviously changed the name of a play he already had to capitalize on the popularity of the radio program.

The plot of the play is typical of several others that Names wrote, especially where there are rich people who are incapable of running their companies and unscrupulous people trying to take advantage of the situation. In this case a new insecticide has been invented and a competing businessman is trying to get it. Amos and Andy are ex-con safecrackers who are hired to get into the safe where the formula is kept.

Though the script does not say so, one can assume that actors performed Amos and Andy in blackface makeup. These characters fit just about every stereotype of African Americans at the time. The two characters refer to themselves as "shines," as do some of the other characters, and they are often referred to as colored boys or "colored bums." They try to avoid work at all costs and frequently mispronounce words, saying "insect suicide" for "insecticide," for example. Gambling and razors, assumed to be black vices, appear throughout the play. Still, this play has some interesting comments about the role of women, as when the female lead says, "In these modern days, A LADY IN DISTRESS, is wont to do her own fighting."[15]

Another topical play was titled *The Return of the Devil* and sometimes *The Call of the Nude*. The script submitted for copyright was titled *The Return of the Devil*, but the headings on acts 2 and 3 are *The Call of the Nude*. It was written for presentation in the 1934 season. Names clearly claims authorship of this play even though he seemed to deny it in other cases. In the Names papers an undated advertising brochure for this play includes a puzzling statement at the bottom: "Art Names has leased this remarkable play for the States of Texas, Oklahoma, Kansas and Colorado."[16]

The plot is a variation of *Faust*, in which a character sells his soul to the devil, except that in this case the devil comes back to earth for two weeks. The plot involves an unhappy and bored wife who has fallen under the influence of a Rasputin-like character who has convinced her they should found a new religion—nudism. The play involves some people who hide money, a very handicapped woman, and a depressed husband about to commit suicide. The devil, in the form of the butler, manipulates the action.

At the end the devil gives Evelyn (another Eve?) an apple and a debate ensues between Evelyn and her boyfriend about eating it. Eventually she does convince him to eat it. The play ends on an ambiguous note. The Bible is quoted quite often in this play, and it is clear that Names knew much about the Bible even though he was not very religious. The character representing the devil makes many references to his background, which the other characters—and probably the audiences—miss.[17]

This is one of the better written plays and shows a good deal of creativity on Names's part, even though the idea of the devil coming to earth is an old one. In advertising, he claimed it was "the play the whole world is talking about," "a comedy-drama written against the present nudist craze that is sweeping the nation." Actually, the play never opposes the nudist fad, despite the fact that Names advertised it that way.[18]

One of the more popular plays during the Whisenhunt era, probably second only to *Are You a Monkey?*, was the melodrama *Deep in the Heart of Texas*. Three versions of this play existed, according to Names family sources, but only one script has been found, and it is under the title *Marquita*. Jean

PEOPLE'S PLAYWRIGHT

Names mentioned that it also was performed under the title *Ramona*.[19] There is no copyright date or any other indication of when it was written, but in reading the script one can infer that it was written sometime in the 1920s: one of the characters, a Mexican strongman, is named Carranza, which was also the name of the president of Mexico during the late 1910s and early 1920s.

One of the scripts is a four-act version and the other two are three-act plays. One version was rewritten to cut two female parts, as Names was often short of women actors. The play is set somewhere near the Mexican border and includes some interesting characters such as a mystery man, Don Marquis, and a bumbling sheriff who sells tombstones and is clearly the G-String character, or comedy relief. As in other Names plays some characters are not aware of their true parentage, but this is revealed in the end and all is well. The bad guys get their just deserts and the innocent are vindicated. The play has much emotional melodrama but also a light touch, as in most of Names's plays.[20]

Names produced a number of plays with political content. In some instances he may have written what his rural audiences wanted to hear, but most of his political comments were probably his own views. Most of Names's plays, even the silliest farces, contained social and political comments, but these were only incidental to the plays.

A few surviving scripts are more clearly political and, unlike those mentioned above, these often were advertised as political vehicles. Names's political plays revolve around war—World War I and the coming World War II. Some of the comments in these plays clearly reflect Names's own war experience and his fear of what was coming, especially after 1939.

The script *We, Who Are Fools* is undated but clearly was written after 1936 since one of the characters refers to the king of England giving up his throne. The play involves a weak husband whose wife is sought after by the local unscrupulous banker and candidate for governor, who is aware she is married. It also includes twin sons, as well as a male lead who has a twin.

Names's political views are quite obvious in this play. John, the male lead who quotes mostly liberal and Democratic ideas, says, "We are built in the likeness of God and are yet the dumbest of all God's creatures for we starve in the midst of plenty and are bankrupt in the midst of prosperity." Andrew, the local banker and candidate for governor, is a Republican, and he makes some serious attacks on Franklin Roosevelt and the New Deal, referring to "Dear Old Santa Clause Roosevelt."

Some of the dialogue in this play and the circumstances of the characters reflect some aspects of Names's own run for governor of Kansas. Mona, the female lead, raises questions throughout about whether the government and its leaders have responsibility for the weak and poor. Joe, the aggressive twin of John, is somewhat cynical when he says, "Elections my dear fellow go to the man who makes the best promises and spends the most money." John was very emphatic about who should serve in government, saying, "NO MAN IS FIT TO BE GOVERNOR! That's the whole thing in a nutshell. That's it. That's the truth. That's what's the matter with our government right now. NO MAN IS FIT TO BE GOVERNOR."

Names railed against both political parties in his political writings, and he follows this practice in a speech by John as well: "Political parties which accept campaign contributions from crooks and honest men alike and who give political jobs as rewards for service without regard for service and who spend the Nations [sic] Money to repair their Political Fences with no regard for national welfare, as both Republicans and Democrats have always done, cannot ever produce a satisfactory government."

One of Names's own campaign promises appears in one of John's speeches. John says if he were governor he would turn the executive branch over to a committee of twelve men and would vote only in case of a tie. Names said in his campaign for governor that coordination and cooperation were the only things that could save the country from ruin, and these same ideas inform the dialogue in the play.

There is a lot of Art Names in this play. Clearly Names was affected significantly by having twins since he creates two sets of twin male characters and gives one set the same names as his own twin sons. At one point he has John say, "All men are twins—the man he is and the man he might have been." Names makes John an aviator in World War I, as Names himself was. John explains, "When I enlisted in the Army I left College where I was studying to be a Lawyer"—also like Names.

The play also reflects Names's philosophy and attitude about marriage. A character talks about being married for fifteen years to a woman who does not love him. The marriage between Art and Maurine lasted fifteen years. Names, the playwright, has Mona ask, "Must a woman be bound forever by a single mistake?" The character of John is not bitter, but he seems to wonder how he could live with a woman that long and not know she was unhappy and possibly never loved him at all.

The trouble between Art and Maurine may well have revolved around Art's lack of ambition to make money. Likewise, in this play John is a dreamer and a person who cares little for money. John says, "I didn't want to sell my soul

PEOPLE'S PLAYWRIGHT

and happiness just to make money." John admits that he does not have much ambition—at least until he reforms at the end of the play. He says, "I've been too soft. Too easy. I never wanted to hurt anyone. I've just drifted. You're right about me. I'm a DREAMER and not a DOER."[21]

Another play, *The Challenge*, has not been found, but surviving advertising material prepared by Names summarizes its content. Names called it "his masterpiece of realistic comedy-drama," and the advertising states that poverty, disease, crime, injustice, and war must end. "Art Names dares the Christian and other decent people of this nation to live by the Golden rule for twenty years," the advertising says. "Christianity is a he-man doctrine. In its fullest sense it has never been tried. The Golden Rule is workable." This corresponds to the theme of cooperation and coordination he used in his gubernatorial campaign: "Art Names says the Golden Rule plus co-operation and co-ordination of our powers—just plain application of ordinary common sense—will solve every question which is troubling the world to-day. It is the basis upon which Catholics and Protestants and those of no denomination can unite—no religious doctrine, just the application of the golden rule." He drops in a bit of philosophy:

> **Poverty will end**
> **We don't need comminism [sic]**
> **We don't need socialism**
> **We don't need facism [sic]**
> **We don't need nazism**
> **Dictators come and go—but right marches on—**[22]

Another play for which only the title exists, *Here Comes the Dictator!*, was also quite political. Again some of the undated advertising is all that remains, offering a tantalizing hint at what the play was about. The flyer explains that two brothers went into the trenches of World War I to make the world safe for democracy. They react in opposite ways in the aftermath of the war, "one of them determined more than ever to fight the cause of Democracy—the other one, bitter and dis-illusioned, determined to smash the ones who had sent him out to kill and be killed while they stayed safely home and raked in their millions!"

The cynical brother sneers at the weaknesses and frailties of his fellow men and fights his way to the top, crushing all opposition, including the president, the Congress, and the Supreme Court. "He hated and despised all politicians—they were the men who once sent him to war but they would never send him to war again—next time he would send them to war!"

Another flyer says that the play was written by an ex-soldier and "is as important a document on the highway that leads to Liberty and freedom as is the Declaration of Independence." It is "a play which marks the road which leads to war, and points the way which leads to peace!" Names warns the potential audience, "You won't have to go to the next war; the next war will come to you—its on the way here now."[23]

Names's family remembered two other political plays with affection but were unable to recall the plots.[24] One was called *The Fighting Fool* and the other *Loop-Legged and Lucky.* The editor of the local newspaper in Meadow, Texas, the *Meadow Star,* who commented on these plays was conscious of their political nature and a bit concerned about audience reaction: "Whatever you may think about Art Names political views you will want to see his two famous political plays 'The Fighting Fool' and 'Loop-Legged and Lucky.'" The editor claimed these were without a doubt two of the funniest plays ever written and that audiences at both plays were in constant roars of laughter. "These wonderful plays are written in a manner which brings delight to both young and old, no matter what their political ideas may be." The editor could not say enough good about Names and his plays: "Yet funny as they were, throughout both of them ran a vein of truth which made a tremendous impression upon the audience." The concluding remarks were ones any showman would relish: "Art Names company has played exactly forty-seven plays here in the past ten years and it was universally agreed that The Fighting Fool and Loop-Legged and Lucky are the two best plays he has ever presented here."[25]

At least one other surviving play, *Lest We Forget,* contains political comments that reflect Names's own opinions. This play covers the period from about 1916 before American entry into World War I through the period prior to World War II. One of the characters is a banker who profiteers on both wars; another character is a young man who is shell-shocked in World War I. The lead character is a teacher who served in World War I and became disillusioned about why the United States entered.

As in all of Names's plays, the characters are drawn very broadly. The actors were expected to develop their characters. The characters in all of his plays are somewhat naive and accept startling events rather casually.

The lead character, Richard, is very critical of bankers and rich people in general. He tells his uncle, "My conscience even hurts me when I have to

teach the little children how to figure interest in school." When the draft begins, he tells the uncle that he wants the government to draft money just as it
is drafting men. The uncle, the character who profits from war, is outraged
and replies, "If the government DRAFTED money, it would deprive the owners
of the use of it as long as the war lasted—why perhaps for two or three years
and during a war is the very best time to invest your money to make more
money." Richard is not sympathetic, "But the Government is going to deprive
me of my life for two or three years—PERHAPS FOREVER."

Richard's antiwar sentiment comes out when he says, "As I understand
you, in order to save DEMOCRACY we will have to kill a few million men and
produce a few MILLIONAIRES out of the profit of that killing." Later he says,
"I hope that those of us who are fortunate enough to get back from this war
alive will have sense enough to fix things so that in the next war nobody will
be able to make millions of dollars while OUR SONS ARE OUT THERE AT THE
FRONT BEING SHOT TO PIECES." He goes on: "The HOPE of the FUTURE lies
not in MONEY but in the proper education and training of our young people
Mr. Moran. This WAR has shaken our MORAL structure to it's [sic] very founda-
tion. We have discovered that some of our most cherished BELIEFS were only
VAIN delusions." In another instance he says, "UNLESS WE BUILD DEMOCRACY
UPON SOMETHING MORE SECURE THAN THE DOLLAR MARK I AM AFRAID THAT
IN ANOTHER GENERATION DEMOCRACY WILL DISAPPEAR." He is rather pessimistic when he says, "Yes, Mr. Moran, we won the war but I am very much
afraid we have lost our souls."

About the coming second war, Richard says, "The United States is now
getting ready to BREED the DOGS OF WAR. And having BRED them we are going
to find they are expensive to FEED, HARD to KILL and even harder still to
CONTROL. We must be careful that in seeking to destroy the enemies of DE-
MOCRACY that we do not build up a war machine which will become a FRAN-
KENSTEIN and in turn destroy the very DEMOCRACY which we sought to save."
Later he says, "I am not in favor of fighting that next war until ALL OF THE
PROFIT IS TAKEN OUT OF WAR AND THE PREPARATION FOR WAR." When the
shell-shocked character is dying in his delusion, he says, "Let's see, what was
we fighting for anyway?" This leaves most everyone else speechless.[26]

Sixteen other scripts survive that have not been discussed here. Some are
about people who are very rich and sometimes lose their money; some are
about poor people who become wealthy. There are criminals and other evil
characters in some of the plays. Often there are brothers, who sometimes do
not know about each other. Some of the plays of this type include *The Crook*,

A Thoroughbred Tramp, The Ghost of "Hank" Watkins, Her Surplus Husband, The Jailbird, and *Nobody Home.*

Quite a few of the plays are simple comedies without much plot. Many of them have a Toby or G-String character who is the butt of jokes but often proves to be smarter than anyone believes and becomes the hero in the end. Two examples are *The Town Marshall* and *The Old Home Town.*

Several of the plays deal with children, sometimes twins, sometimes brothers who are lost and then found during the play. Three examples are *Dad's Other Son, Too Many Babies,* and *Twin Babies.*

Some of the plays are set in the American West. In addition to *Deep in the Heart of Texas,* there are plays such as *Under Arizona Skies* and *The Game.* These plays always involve some sort of intrigue, such as a mortgage about to be foreclosed or a villain trying to steal the ranch. Some of the plays, such as *The Billion Dollar Ransom* and *Who Done It,* also known as *I Love a Mystery,* are typical mystery plays, but often the plots are simple and audiences must have had to suspend credulity to appreciate the performance.

The content of Names's plays reflects the time in which they were written. Racial and ethnic stereotypes appear regularly, but they did not create much of a stir, or even a ripple, among audiences or else they would not have been there. Names was writing white plays for white audiences. Using race for a laugh was common in the theater until the 1950s, so Names's work is not unusual.

Names's plays should not be criticized for what they are not but instead judged for what they are. They were original—even if Names was inspired by similar plays. They were written for a specific time and place. His plays might be trite and excessively melodramatic by today's standards, but they did what they were designed to do—they entertained.

EIGHT

Road's End

THE NAMES-WHISENHUNT PARTNERSHIP COULD NOT HAVE lasted indefinitely. Numerous obstacles lay in the way of a long-term association, and as events developed, it was rather short-lived.

The vicissitudes of operating a traveling tent show were significant. The war presented several problems such as rationing of critical materials that made the operation uncertain from day to day. Rubber and gasoline rationing limited the distances the show could travel, and sugar shortages threatened the availability of candy and syrup for snow cones. Other shortages and rationed goods forced Names and Whisenhunt to improvise. During the war, people had more money than before and were anxious to get the goods they had been denied for so long. To some people in small towns, the traveling tent show seemed somewhat backward and old-fashioned; these people were using their new wealth to drive—when rationing allowed them to do so—to larger towns where there were greater opportunities for entertainment and more consumer products available. Even though the government attempted to control prices, a degree of inflation crept into the economy. Names and Whisenhunt felt they should raise the admission and concession prices for their show, but they feared that the small towns would not tolerate raises; they did all they could to hold expenses down, but that became more difficult as time passed.[1]

The hindrances were serious, but they were not enough to stop the operation. Names was familiar with and accustomed to the problems of travel, but for Whisenhunt, it was a new experience. He had always been a man willing to take chances, but the continued uncertainty of life on the road was taking its toll on his morale. The constant threat of storms was another uncertainty. Even though the Names-Whisenhunt operation had not encountered a disastrous storm that put them out of business, some of those they encountered caused periods of closure while repairs were made. Every night the show did not operate was a loss—

and any loss was significant to a business operating on such a low margin and with limited resources to fall back upon.[2]

Another problem Whisenhunt faced was his wife's attitude about the show. When the troupe was on the road, she refused to travel all season, using the excuse that she had a small child at home; she really did not like the show life very much. She always had some reservations because she was very religious and wondered about the morality of a tent show. Mostly, she did not like the economic uncertainty and the constant moving. She liked to stay home and to have each day predictable, and Whisenhunt was not comfortable when his wife was not with him. She did come to visit often and seemed to enjoy those times; but they were more like a vacation, not a way of life, and she could not visualize doing this indefinitely.[3]

Another factor that caused Whisenhunt's enthusiasm to weaken somewhat was the absence of his eldest son. Junior Whisenhunt had originally been the one who was so excited about being a part of the show, but now he was in the military and away from the show. The other boys, Kenneth and Lewis, loved traveling and being a part of the show, but the infectious enthusiasm of Junior was missing. Whisenhunt could also see the end of war coming; with the increasing popularity of motion pictures and other forms of entertainment, he wondered what the future of the tent show would be. It had succeeded during the war years, but would it survive the postwar era?[4]

During the last months of 1944 Whisenhunt considered getting out of the show and finding some other way of making a living. Since his real love was running a pool hall, he wondered if he would be able to reopen his business when the war was over or whether the officials of Terry County would be uncooperative with him.

The determining event for Whisenhunt and the beginning of the end for Names came on December 2, 1944, in the town of Muleshoe, Texas. Muleshoe had been good town for Names for many years. Business had been good on the road that season, and Names and Whisenhunt had decided to stay out as long as they could. Now the weather was getting cold, and it was time to get back to winter quarters as heating the tent was becoming more difficult.

Whisenhunt's wife and the youngest Whisenhunt son, who was in the first grade, came to Muleshoe since it was about seventy-five miles from Meadow. Muleshoe was to be the last stop before coming back to Meadow, and she was anxious to see her husband and sons. She was also interested in seeing a play, a new version of the Jesse James story as written by Names, since her son Kenneth played the role of Bob Ford, the man who shot Jesse James. Beulah

ROAD'S END

Whisenhunt and the youngest child were there for the new play. No one knew it at the time, but the Jesse James play was to be the last performance of the Names-Whisenhunt partnership.[5]

Fires on traveling tent shows were common. Tents were canvas, made of cotton, hemp, or flax, and were extremely flammable, and the process of fire-proofing them was primitive at best. Maurine Names said that in the more prosperous days of the show, in the 1920s, they had a fire-resistant tent, which cost about four hundred dollars more than a regular tent, an enormous sum for the period. Even so, the tent was not fireproof. "Fire resistant" simply meant that instead of "flaming and going up whoosh all at once, it just eats along and gives you a little more time." During the Names-Whisenhunt period, the tent was a makeshift operation, a combination of Names's old tent and a second tent added to make it longer—a structure that was not fire resistant.[6]

There was a way of trying to make the tent fire resistant, but it was a dangerous process using a mixture of gasoline and paraffin.[7] The paraffin was melted in a bucket on a Coleman gas stove, gasoline was poured in it, and the mixture was then dipped out of the bucket and thrown across the top of the tent. The idea of putting gasoline on an open fire was a frightening prospect, at best, but with inexperienced people it could be disastrous. Jack Names remembered: "My God, that was hazardous. It was great, great waterproofing, but it was hazardous as hell!"[8] The tent that was standing in Muleshoe had been treated with the mixture some time earlier. No one ever assumed that the treatment would really work.

On the fateful night, Bill Whisenhunt went to the tent an hour or so before the show was scheduled to open to light the heaters as he did every night. The Coleman space heaters, which burned kerosene with a mixture of air, had connections where manual pumps were attached to pump air into the mixture. As the stoves were lighted, air was pumped in to give the fire a mixture that produced a blue flame.[9] Sometimes the stoves did not work well, especially when they were old, and the air blew out. If the valve was not closed quickly, gasoline would come out also and fire would blow out of the heater.[10]

That was what happened when Bill Whisenhunt began lighting the stoves in the tent. One of the stoves blew out and spewed fire on the sidewall of the tent. When some of the fire hit Whisenhunt and caught his heavy woolen coat on fire, he immediately ran up the aisle toward the stage with his coat burning. He later said he was going to the backstage area to find a blanket to wrap around himself to put out the flame. His son Kenneth, who was coming down

TENT SHOW

the aisle just as his father started running in his direction, threw him to the ground and rolled him in the dirt until the fire was out. In the meantime the fire had spread from the sidewall up to the top of the tent. After his father's fire was extinguished, Kenneth ran to the back of the tent and found Art Names shaving in anticipation of the night's performance. Kenneth yelled to tell him that the tent was on fire. By this time, people outside the tent were aware of the fire, and there was much shouting and activity around the tent.[11]

Art ran into the tent to see what was going on, his straight razor still in his hand. Jack had come into the tent by this time, and he and his father began to drop the center poles of the tent. Names worked as fast as he could from under the tent to cut it into two pieces with his razor, hoping that the two sides would fall apart so he might be able to save at least half of the tent. Jack recalled that his father was cutting panels out of the top of the tent while it was lying on the ground with only the side poles standing. Jack said, "I can remember the fire when that blue flame leaped across. It just leaped sections that were three feet wide. I can still remember from that old Coleman stove that there was a stream of flaming gas spurting out."[12] Art and Jack were working frantically underneath the tent when "all of a sudden everything underneath caught fire at the same time and the flame went 'phew' the whole length of the tent."[13] Jack said the flame never touched them, but his father decided it was too dangerous and he told Jack to get out from under the tent. Both of them got out before the flames consumed the entire tent. Jack said, "I can still remember that a sheet of bluish fire came at me. It was really strange."[14]

The fire did its work very fast. Maurine later said it took only seven minutes. She said they had been burned out completely four times, but this was the worst because now they could afford to lose the show the least.[15] One of the ironies of this incident was that the tent was located directly across the street from the Muleshoe Volunteer Fire Department, but the fire engine did not get to the tent until the worst damage was done. People who remembered the event recalled that when the door to the fire station was opened, the fire engine had a flat tire.[16] When Art Names submitted his tax return for 1944, he attached a letter describing the fire and the financial losses and explained that the fire department did not get to the fire because the firemen could not get the fire engine started. It arrived in time to help clean up after the damage was done.[17]

The damage to the show was almost total. The tent, which they had enlarged in 1944 to more than a hundred feet long and double sidewalled, was a complete loss. Names explained to the Internal Revenue Service the spe-

ROAD'S END

cifics of the loss. The electric light bulbs on the front of the tent, in the auditorium, and on the stage were a complete loss, and the wiring and electrical fixtures on the inside of the tent were about a 75 percent loss. Not many of the 450 wooden folding chairs—which had cost Names and Whisenhunt $18 per dozen new, plus freight—were destroyed, but they were partially burned and warped and were worth about 50 percent less after the fire. The poles were about 50 percent damaged. Names said they saved quite a bit of the candy and prizes, "but the fire department got there in time to throw water all over them and we had a heavy damage that way and the crowd which collected to see the fire stole lots of candy and prizes." The picture screen, front curtain, all the scenery, a big rug, and all the stage rigging were destroyed. The fire department did keep the stage from burning by driving the truck on which the stage was located from under the burning tent. It sustained some damage but was not destroyed. The marquee and proscenium were destroyed, as was one wardrobe trunk and all the loose wardrobe on the stage and in the dressing rooms. Some manuscripts also burned.

Names claimed a loss on his tax return of $100 for the company and $425 for himself individually. He was specific with the Internal Revenue Service about the losses and wrote letters in a conversational fashion as if he and the tax officials were old friends.[18]

The fire was a devastating blow to both Names and Whisenhunt. They had been just getting by as it was, and now most of what they had was gone.[19] They loaded up what was left and went on to Meadow to decide what the next step would be. Whisenhunt took this opportunity to tell Names that he had been thinking of trying something else; now the fire had made the decision for him. He offered to sell what was remaining of his share of the show to Names, and Names agreed. The records are not clear about whether Names had the money to pay Whisenhunt his share, but it seems unlikely. Probably he promised to pay Whisenhunt as soon as he could, and, undoubtedly, he paid the debt, which was very small after the fire.[20] The parting was friendly, and the two men remained close friends.

Names went to Leuders, Texas, where he opened a new tent show. In a letter to the Internal Revenue Service in March, 1945, he explained, "When our outfit burned last December, my partner got cold feet (or maybe it was hot feet) and decided that he had had enough of the tent show business—so he took his truck and went home—"[21] He explained that he had "an old junk skating rink tent that I bought out at Meade, Kansas—$125 for the tent and $32.50 for transportation—I tried to buy a good used tent but the cheapest I could get offered me was $600.00 and that didn't include poles or side-walls."[22]

His motion picture machine had been saved from the fire, so Names had a way to offer entertainment to local residents. He knew the people of Leuders and hoped they would respond favorably to his much-reduced operation. He refurbished the equipment he had left from the fire by sanding and varnishing the poles and folding chairs that survived and building new bench seating to fill in the gaps caused by the fire losses. In February, 1945, he wrote a friend in Boise City, Oklahoma, a young girl he had known from playing the town previously. She was one of many people, quite a few of them young women, with whom he corresponded on a regular basis after his divorce in 1939. He was getting ready to get his new tent operating. "I surely have been busy now here—Varnishing the chairs and painting all the poles etc.—but I have the old outfit looking right nice again now—" This was the last letter she received from Names; she cherished it and kept it for many years after his death.[23]

Names actually was able to open two motion picture operations, one in Leuders and the other in the town of McAdoo, Texas. Art and Jean were in Leuders getting the tent operational and the show open, while Maurine and Jack opened the show in McAdoo and tried to make a success of it. Maurine did not stay long; she and her husband left, leaving Jack alone to run the show. Jack said he was "just eking out a living" and sometimes not making enough in admissions to meet expenses and to provide food for himself.[24]

Jean had a better time of it in Leuders, partly because he was with his father, enjoying what he felt were some of the better times they had together. "I actually spent more time with him that year. I was isolated with him and we got to know each other pretty well."[25] Jean said, "He was interesting to talk with and his interests were so broad that he was never dull or boring."[26]

Despite the hard times, Names seemed to be getting back on his feet. Always an inveterate letter writer, he kept in touch with his former partner and friend, Bill Whisenhunt, in Meadow and told him how he was dealing with the various problems, especially the challenges of the war that was still under way.

With the Whisenhunts back in Meadow and out of the show, Bill Whisenhunt was faced with the serious matter of finding some other livelihood so he could provide for his family. He apparently had a little money put away and did not have to get a job or open a business immediately.

Beulah Whisenhunt was very worried about her son Junior who was fighting the Japanese in the Philippines. She also missed her family—her mother, brothers, and sisters—who had gone to California at the beginning of the war to take advantage of the job opportunities in defense industries. Because she was at loose ends and restless, her husband told her he thought she should go to California to visit her family. He would follow in a few weeks if he did not find some work or business in Meadow before then. He knew he could always find work in California because of the great demands of the war effort.

Beulah, Kenneth, and the youngest son, Donald, went to California in early 1945. Donald enrolled in first grade in Richmond, California, for the month, approximately, that they were there. Bill Whisenhunt and the third son, Lewis, remained in Meadow. While his wife was gone, Whisenhunt bought a gasoline station on the main intersection in Meadow. Beulah and the two boys returned in about a month, and their lives went back to a more normal arrangement.[27]

After Names was established in Leuders and Whisenhunt had his gasoline station running smoothly, the government notified the family of the death of Junior Whisenhunt in the Philippines. The devastation for the Whisenhunt family was obvious, but the Names family was affected more strongly than one might have expected. They had known Junior for perhaps as much as ten years, but for a few of those years he had been active on the show and had made an impression on them.[28]

During the fall of 1945, when Whisenhunt heard that Names was ill, he immediately went to Leuders to check on his old friend. He found Names in the hospital in the nearby town of Stamford. Whisenhunt never knew exactly what was wrong with Names. Names told him that he had had a craving for a persimmon, a tropical fruit edible only when it is completely ripe. Names said he wanted it too much, and he had eaten the persimmon before it was fully ripe. He thought this was the problem and that it was not serious. They had a pleasant visit, and since Names seemed to be doing all right, Whisenhunt returned to Meadow to his own obligations.

Shortly after Whisenhunt's return to Meadow, he received word that Names had died in the hospital in Stamford on November 8, 1945. Whisenhunt, who did not have a reliable automobile large enough for his family, arranged with a neighbor to drive his family to Stamford for the funeral.[29]

The official cause of death as reported by the attending physician was coronary occlusion thrombosis, or a blood clot that blocked the heart artery and caused the death of the heart muscle. This was probably a guess on the part of the doctor since no autopsy was performed and the physician did not know Names very well, having attended him only from October 10 until his death.[30] Probably the doctor knew that Names had a heart condition, although Whisenhunt was not told when he visited Names in the hospital. Names, who was just five days short of his fifty-fourth birthday, was mourned by friends and family because they loved him and because the promise of the future was cut so short.

Jack Names, who was running the show in McAdoo, was devastated by news of his father's heart attack. To make matters worse, the family (presumably Maurine and Jean) wanted him to stay where he was because they felt he could not do anything and needed to keep the show running. When he was informed of Art's death, Jack said he had "a strange reaction," though it was probably normal for a teenage boy. He said, "I danced all night in the sagebrush and stuff, you know. That's how I felt about it. I didn't cry or anything, but I just danced a very painful dance all night. I was exhausted in the morning. The sun came up and I went and laid down and went to bed. I was all alone. I knew that."

Jack thought his father knew the end was near. He said his father was in the process of adjusting to the changed situation after the end of the Whisenhunt partnership and was "trying to set up things to get his kids through school when he died. For them to have a way to support themselves." He was working hard and was concerned about the twins' finishing high school. Jack said, "I think he knew something was coming off. I think he knew he was going to die because he had said it once to Maurine's Slim. I think he knew his time was limited." Jack later thought his father had been having chest pains, indigestion, and other symptoms of a heart condition but did not tell anyone.[31]

The funeral was held in Leuders, and the burial was in Highland Cemetery in Stamford, Texas, on November 11, 1945, Armistice Day, the date that marked the end of fighting in World War I.[32]

After Names's death, Jean wanted Jack to close the operation in McAdoo and come to Leuders and work with him on the show that he and Art had been running. Jack said that Jean began to have chest pains after his father's death, and "he thought he was having a heart attack. He thought he was going to die like Dad did, you know." Jean was upset enough that Jack agreed to close the McAdoo operation and join Jean in Leuders.[33]

The boys had just turned eighteen years old when their father died. They worked together in Leuders, and Jean finished working his way through high school. Jack later completed high school in the military through the United States Armed Forces Institute program. The boys were almost destitute.

When Jean finished high school, the boys closed the show and joined the armed forces. The war was over, but there was still a need for people in the military, and they entered in time to qualify for benefits under the GI Bill of Rights. When they came out of military service, they went to different colleges in Abilene, Texas, Jean to Hardin-Simmons University, a Baptist institution, and Jack to Abilene Christian College, a college run by the Church of Christ.

Amazingly, both boys obtained educations that allowed them to have professional careers. After growing up as they did, being raised for several years by foster parents, attending many schools in a year, dropping out for a time to get the show operational, and then making up the lost time, they were unlikely candidates for even finishing high school. As it turned out, Jean got a master's degree in business and became an instructor in a community college in Los Angeles. Jack went to medical school and became a medical doctor, specializing in pediatrics.[34]

As for the Whisenhunts, they would vividly remember the few years of association with Art Names and his show for the rest of their lives. Whisenhunt operated the gas station in Meadow for about two years, but he was not happy in this role. Wartime rationing and other restrictions were still on for a few months after the war was over, and he had a difficult time coping with the regulations and staying on the right side of the law since there was such an active black market in ration stamps. He was always looking for new opportunities and saw the gas station as a temporary activity.

In 1947 Whisenhunt got his chance to reopen his pool hall. County officials had no logical excuse not to go back to the arrangement that had existed before the war, so they came to an understanding. Whisenhunt bought a building in the business section of Meadow and converted it to a pool hall and domino parlor. He opened at a propitious time; prosperity continued after the war even though many people, Whisenhunt included, strongly feared that the country would return to the depression. That did not happen, and Whisenhunt took advantage of the situation.

In the late 1940s and 1950s the Whisenhunts went back into show business, showing motion pictures. Whisenhunt's oldest surviving son, Kenneth, who had not finished high school and was looking for some way to make a living, was influenced by the association with Names so much that he wanted to do something similar. He convinced his father, and they bought a new tent. They erected it on a vacant lot next to the pool hall and operated during the fall months, the time of the cotton harvest in West Texas when there were so many migrant workers in the region. They used Junior's trailer house as the ticket booth and projection room and showed motion pictures in the tent.

Since so many of the migrant workers were Spanish-speaking residents of Texas from the Rio Grande Valley area, the Whisenhunts began to show Spanish-language movies.

They were doing so well with the pool hall and the tent show that they expanded again around 1950. Whisenhunt bought another business building down the street from the pool hall, and Kenneth converted it to a movie theater. There they showed both English- and Spanish-languages films but eventually concentrated almost exclusively on movies in Spanish. Whisenhunt hired a man to run the pool hall for him at night while he and his youngest son, Donald, who was eleven years old, ran the show (since the third son, Lewis, had enlisted in the U.S. Army in 1948 after he graduated from high school). Whisenhunt sold tickets and took care of business generally, and Donald was the projectionist and managed the popcorn machine.

While Whisenhunt and Donald were running the show in Meadow, the family moved the tent to a crossroads village named Lakeview about twenty miles east of Meadow where a cotton gin and a small grocery store were located. Whisenhunt and Kenneth scouted the area and found that many migrant workers passed through this area and bought groceries in the store; in addition, migrant housing was nearby. The Whisenhunts decided that this would be a good place for the show and made arrangements to use the land behind the store for erecting the tent. Kenneth Whisenhunt and his mother operated it every night, showing the same films that were shown in Meadow.

The three businesses were successful enough that, in 1951, Whisenhunt was able to build a new house for the family, using lumber from the building he had bought in downtown Meadow and then dismantled. Used lumber was adequate for the house's outside walls, which were then covered with stucco. The family continued to play movies in the tent, which they erected beside the pool hall, and the business did fairly well despite competition from movie theaters in nearby towns.[35] Whisenhunt had achieved his goals of having a family, supporting that family, and rising above the economic and social level of his parents. And the Whisenhunts had benefited, clearly, from their association with Names.

Bill Whisenhunt did not survive much longer. In the fall of 1951 he was hospitalized for an extended period when he had a gallbladder attack and suffered periods of hallucinations during his stay. After his emergency surgery for a ruptured gallbladder, the problems with hallucinations ended. While recovering from the surgery in the hospital, he suffered what was first diagnosed as a heart attack. The doctors later revised their diagnosis and indicated that it was not as serious as a heart attack. When he returned home, he began a slow and steady recovery, but it was not to be sustained.

On February 24, 1952, he died of a heart attack while on a farm near Lubbock, Texas. His son Kenneth and a friend rushed Whisenhunt to the hospital in Lubbock, but Whisenhunt was dead when they arrived. He was fifty-six years old.[36]

Now the two principals in the wartime partnership were both gone. The memories of show business and life on the road were more meaningful for the Names family because they had lived the life much longer, but the experience was significant for the Whisenhunts as well. Despite this, neither family continued in show business, with one exception. When Art, Jr., returned from the war, he tried acting, but when that was not successful, he became a sound mixer for motion pictures and spent the rest of his career in that craft.

The Nameses and the Whisenhunts lost contact in the years after Art's death, and their relationships were not reestablished until thirty years later in 1975. Still, the memory of Art Names was constantly evoked in the Whisenhunt household long after he was dead. His failures as a family man aside, Names had kept the tent show tradition alive and had lived his own life fully. Art Names represented one man's personal search for the American dream. Few would argue that he did not succeed.

NOTES

INTRODUCTION

1. John Quincy Adams quoted in Constance Rourke, *The Roots of American Culture* (New York: Harcourt Brace and Company, 1942), pp. 4–5.

2. Ibid., p. 6.

3. Ibid., p. 9.

4. Plato, *Republic*, Book 10, translated by Benjamin Jowett (New York: Co-Operative Publication Society, 1901), p. 299ff.

5. Licensing Act of 1737 as quoted by Kenneth D. Wright, "Henry Fielding and the Theatres Act of 1737," *Quarterly Journal of Speech* (Oct., 1964): 253.

6. Tertullian, On the Spectacles, translated by Reverend S. Thelwall, in *The Writings of Septimus Florens Tertullian*, vol. 1 (Edinburgh: T. & T. Clark, 1869).

7. Philip C. Lewis, *Trouping: How the Show Came to Town* (New York: Harper and Row, 1973), p. 19.

8. Rourke, *Roots of American Culture*, p. 95.

9. Garff B. Wilson, *Three Hundred Years of American Drama and Theatre* (Englewood Cliffs, N.J.: Prentice Hall, 1973), p. 8.

10. Gilbert Seldes, "The People and the Arts," in Bernard Rosenberg and David Manning White, *Mass Culture: The Popular Arts in America* (Glencoe, Ill.: Free Press, 1957), p. 75.

11. Sol Smith, *Theatrical Management in the West and South* (New York: Harper and Row, Publishers, 1868), and Noah M. Ludlow, *Dramatic Life as I Found It* (St. Louis: G. I. Jones and Company, 1880).

12. Junius Brutus Booth, father of Edwin and John Wilkes Booth, reportedly willed his entire wardrobe to John Wilkes, deeply hurting his son Edwin, who had cared for and shepherded him through many of his years as an eccentric, erratic, and flamboyant touring star. The wardrobe was confiscated by the United States government after John Wilkes assassinated Abraham Lincoln.

13. Wilson, *Three Hundred Years*, p. 132.

14. *Encyclopedia Americana*, vol. 23 (New York, Americana Corporation, 1957), p. 174.

15. Walter K. Waters, Jr., "George L. Baker and the Baker Stock Company" (Ph.D. diss., Stanford University, 1964), pp. 48ff.

16. Fay Bainter, interview by W. K. Waters, Palm Springs, Calif., Mar. 11, 1962.

17. Diamond Dye was the commercial name of a popular aniline dye marketed at the end of the nineteenth and well into the twentieth centuries. With the addition of gum arabic the dye could be used to paint muslin panels without having the colors bleed into each other. Such panels were very flexible and

could easily be folded for packing, whereas drops painted with scenic paint tended to be stiff and could only be rolled for transportation, thus requiring the use of a long-bed truck or a railway boxcar. Diamond dye drops were normally used by small touring groups and were standard for tent show presentations. Though Diamond Dye was a commercial name, its use for theater drops was so common that it became an accepted name for such scenic pieces and was consistently referred to in the lower case. The hard scenery used by the large touring companies was composed primarily of flats, wooden frames covered with canvas and painted. Because of the size and structure of this kind of scenery, railroad boxcars were often necessary. In fact, standard scenic pieces were specifically designed to be loaded in and out of a boxcar, the size of the door establishing what became a traditional maximum width for all theater scenic pieces.

18. *Abstract of the 14th Census of the United States* (Washington, D.C.: United States Printing Office, 1923).

19. The Delco system relied on storage batteries charged by a small wind- or motor-driven generator.

20. Walter Prescott Webb, *The Handbook of Texas* (Austin: Texas State Historical Association, 1952), p. 165.

21. *New York Times*, Feb. 21, 22, and 23, 1925.

22. For an outstanding selection of the representative plays of this period, see Kenneth MacGowan and Harold Clurman, *Famous American Plays of the 1920s and 1930s* (Garden City, N.Y.: Fireside Theatre, 1959).

23. Alfred E. Bernstein, *The Business of the Theatre: An Economic History of the American Theatre, 1750–1932* (1932; rpt., New York: Benjamin Bloom, 1964), p. 89.

24. Ibid., p. 100.

25. Further discussions of tent shows, their programs, management, and audiences can be found in Jere C. Mickel, *Footlight on the Prairie* (St. Cloud, Minn.: North Star Press, 1974), and Bernstein, *Business of the Theatre*, pp. 98–100.

26. *New York Times*, July 2, 1961.

CHAPTER 2. REPERTOIRE TENT THEATER IN AMERICA

1. Joe Creason, "Tent Show," *Louisville Courier-Journal Magazine*, July 18, 1948, pp. 5–7.

2. William Lawrence Slout, *Theatre in a Tent: The Development of a Provincial Entertainment* (Bowling Green, Ohio: Popular Press, 1972), p. ix.

3. Laura Bergquist, "Show Business in the Sticks," *Coronet Magazine* 19 (Jan., 1946): pp. 121–23.

4. Slout, *Theatre in a Tent*, p. 10.

5. Ibid., p. 12.

6. Earl Chapin May, "Our Canvas Broadway," *Country Gentleman*, May, 1931, pp. 16, 17, 95; Zelda F. Popkin, "The Tent Show Turns to Sex," *Outlook and Independent* 156 (Sept. 24, 1930): pp. 128–30.

7. Creason, "Tent Show," pp. 5–7; May, "Our Canvas Broadway," pp. 16, 17, 95; Joe Creason, "The Tent Show Carries On," *Louisville Courier-Journal Magazine*, Aug. 20, 1961, pp. 5–7.

8. Herb Walter, *Fifty Years Under Canvas* (Hugo, Okla.: Achme, 1962); Frank A. Waugh, *Outdoor Theatres* (Boston: Richard G. Badger, 1917).

9. Slout, *Theatre in a Tent*, pp. 23–27.

10. Ibid., pp. 35–47.

11. Harry P. Harrison, *Culture Under Canvas: The Story of Tent Chautauqua* (New York: Hastings House, 1958); Charles F. Horner, *Strike the Tents: The Story of Chautauqua* (Philadelphia: Dorrance and Company, 1954).

12. Slout, *Theatre in a Tent*, p. 51.

13. Ibid., p. 52.

14. Winifred Johnson, "Medicine Show," *Southwest Review* 21 (July, 1936): pp. 390–99; May, "Our Canvas Broadway," May, 1931, pp. 16, 17, 95.

15. Harrison, *Culture Under Canvas, passim*; Horner, *Strike the Tents, passim*.

16. Creason, "Tent Show," pp. 5–7; Creason, "Tent Show Carries On," pp. 5–7.

CHAPTER 3. PRAIRIE ORIGINS

1. Mildred B. Stout, *John Hicks, Jr., 1799–1851, and Caroline Fish, 1800–1860: The Ancestors and Descendants* (Pullman, Wash.: privately published, 1983), p. 35; Fred R. Ford to author, Meade, Kans., May 2, 1973; Ruth Stump to author, Colorado Springs, Colo., Oct. 3, 1973; Certificate of Death, Arthur Andrew Names, Stamford, Tex., Nov. 8, 1945, copy in Whisenhunt files.

2. Stump to author, Nov. 3, 1973; Maurine Worthington (former wife of Arthur Names), interview by author, Brea, Calif., Aug. 7, 1975; Milburn Stone, interview by author, North Hollywood, Calif., Aug. 6, 1975.

3. Stone interview; Worthington interview.

4. Stump to author, Apr. 17, 1973, Oct. 3, 1973.

5. Ibid., Oct. 3, 1973.

6. Names to My Dear Sister Violet, Nov. 8, 1939, copy in Whisenhunt files.

7. Beulah King (wife of William A. Whisenhunt), interview by author, Meadow, Tex., July 25, 1975.

8. Stump to author, Oct. 3, 1973.

9. Cleo Akers to author, Dighton, Kans., Apr. 29, 1973.

10. Fred R. Ford to author, Meade, Kans., May 2, 1973.

11. Frank A. Murphy to author, Canon City, Colo., May 22, 1973.

12. For an understanding of Kansas in this era, see Patricia A. Spillman, *The Kansas Ethos in the Last Three Decades of the Nineteenth Century* (Emporia, Kans.: Emporia State University, 1988), and Jeffrey Lostler, *Prairie Populism: The Fate of Agrarian Radicalism in Kansas, Nebraska, and Iowa, 1880–1892* (Lawrence: University Press of Kansas, 1993).

13. For information on White, see Sally Foreman Griffith, *Home Town News:*

William Allen White and the Emporia Gazette (New York: Oxford University Press, 1989).

14. Worthington interview.

15. *McCracken (Kans.) Enterprise*, Dec. 31, 1920.

16. Ibid., Sept. 9, 1907.

17. Robert D. Turvey, assistant registrar, University of Kansas, to author, Feb. 2, 1995.

18. *McCracken (Kans.) Enterprise*, Dec. 20, 1912.

19. Betty Fischer, assistant dean for administration, Washburn School of Law, to author, Topeka, Kans., Jan. 30, 1995.

20. Names, Office of D. E. Hopkins, to Lida Floyd, Lyons, Kans., Feb. 15, 1911, Names Papers.

21. *McCracken (Kans.) Enterprise*, Apr., 1920, quoted in Shirley Higgins and Carolyn Thompson, eds., *McCracken History ... Through Pictures and Newspaper Accounts* (Hays, Kans.: McCracken Centennial Committee, 1987), p. 115.

22. *McCracken (Kans.) Enterprise*, June 11, 1920.

23. Ibid., Dec. 8, 1922.

24. Kenneth Whisenhunt (son of William A. Whisenhunt), interview by author, San Jose and Modesto, Calif., Aug. 10, 1975; Worthington interview; King interview.

25. Carolyn Bennett, Attorney Admissions, Supreme Court of Kansas, to author, Mar. 8, 1995.

26. *McCracken (Kans.) Enterprise*, Aug. 1910, as reported in Higgins and Thompson, *McCracken History*, p. 69.

27. *LaCrosse (Kans.) Republican*, May 3, 1912.

28. *McCracken (Kans.) Enterprise*, May 24, 1912.

29. *McCracken (Kans.) Enterprise*, July, 1912, Nov., 1912, as reported in Higgins and Thompson, *McCracken History*, vol. 2, pp. 77–78; *McCracken (Kans.) Enterprise*, Aug. 23, 1912, Nov. 22, 1912.

30. *McCracken (Kans.) Enterprise*, July, 1913, as reported in Higgins and Thompson, *McCracken History*, p. 82.

31. *McCracken (Kans.) Enterprise*, Aug. 29, 1913.

32. Mrs. Frank Sutton to author, Hoisington, Kans., Apr. 4, 1973.

33. Nancy M. Wilson to author, Mojave, Calif., May 10, 1973.

34. *McCracken (Kans.) Enterprise*, Dec., 1913, Feb., 1917, Apr., 1917, as reported in Higgins and Thompson, *McCracken History*, pp. 84, 98, 99; *McCracken (Kans.) Enterprise*, Dec. 15, 1913; *Ransom (Kans.) Record*, as quoted in *McCracken (Kans.) Enterprise*, Apr. 1, 1917.

35. *McCracken (Kans.) Enterprise*, Oct., 1914, as reported in Higgins and Thompson, *McCracken History*, 87; *McCracken (Kans.) Enterprise*, Nov. 6, 1914, Jan. 1, 1915.

36. *McCracken (Kans.) Enterprise*, Feb. 27, 1914.

37. Council Minutes, City of McCracken Minute Book, Apr. 7, 1915, p. 37.

38. *McCracken (Kans.) Enterprise*, June, 1916, as reported in Higgins and Thompson, *McCracken History*, p. 95; *McCracken (Kans.) Enterprise*, June 16, 1916.

39. *McCracken (Kans.) Enterprise*, Feb., 1917, as reported in Higgins and Thompson, *McCracken History*, p. 98.

40. *Ransom Record* as quoted in *McCracken (Kans.) Enterprise*, Apr. 1, 1917.

41. *McCracken (Kans.) Enterprise*, Aug., 1917, as reported in Higgins and Thompson, *McCracken History*, p. 100.

42. *McCracken (Kans.) Enterprise*, Sept., 1917, as reported in Higgins and Thompson, *McCracken History*, p. 102.

43. Worthington interview; Jack Names (son of Arthur Names), interview by author, Modesto, Calif., Aug. 10, 1975; Jean Names (son of Arthur Names), interview by author, Brea, Calif., Aug. 7, 1975.

44. Names to Lida Floyd, Tacoma, Wash., Jan. 22, 1918, copy provided by Carolyn Thompson, McCracken, Kans.

45. Jack Names interview.

46. *McCracken (Kans.) Enterprise*, Aug., 1918, as reported in Higgins and Thompson, *McCracken History*, p. 112.

47. Council Minutes, City of McCracken Minute Book, Apr. 29, 1919, p. 185.

48. Ibid., May 6, 1919, p. 186.

49. Ibid., p. 187.

50. Ibid., May 16, 1919, p. 188.

51. Ibid., July 16, 1920, p. 233.

52. *McCracken (Kans.) Enterprise*, Sept. 10, 1920, Dec. 31, 1920.

53. *McCracken (Kans.) Enterprise*, Feb., 1921, Dec., 1921, as reported in Higgins and Thompson, *McCracken History*, pp. 120, 124.

54. *McCracken (Kans.) Enterprise*, Jan. 27, 1922.

55. *McCracken (Kans.) Enterprise*, Aug., 1922, as reported in Higgins and Thompson, *McCracken History*, p. 127.

56. *McCracken (Kans.) Enterprise*, Nov., 1922, as reported in Higgins and Thompson, *McCracken History*, p. 128; *McCracken (Kans.) Enterprise*, Nov. 24, 1922.

57. Stone interview.

58. Worthington interview.

59. Ibid.

60. Stone interview.

61. Worthington interview.

62. *McCracken (Kans.) Enterprise*, Feb. 2, 1924.

63. Stout, *John Hicks, Jr.*, 35.

64. Worthington interview; Donald M. Allison to author, Woodward, Okla., May 4, 1973.

65. Worthington interview.

66. Stone interview.

67. Ibid.

68. Ibid.

69. Ibid.

70. Most of this section is based largely on Whisenhunt family oral tradition and

interviews with members of the Whisenhunt family, including Beulah Whisenhunt King, the widow of William Whisenhunt, and sons Kenneth and Lewis Whisenhunt. The information for this section comes from these sources, except where there are specific references and notes to other sources.

71. United States Census, 1870, Fannin County, Tex.

CHAPTER 4. FEAST OR FAMINE

1. Mayme Jones to author, Jetmore, Kans., Aug. 27, 1973.

2. Ibid.

3. Worthington interview; Stone interview.

4. Ibid.

5. "Art Names Company Pleases Public," *Hydro Review*, n.d., Names Papers.

6. Worthington interview.

7. Ibid.

8. *McCracken (Kans.) Enterprise*, Feb., 1924, as reported in Higgins and Thompson, *McCracken History*, 134; *McCracken (Kans.) Enterprise*, Feb. 2, 1924; Stout, 35.

9. Marie Buss to author, Hugoton, Kans., June 1, 1973.

10. Worthington interview.

11. M. L. Tooley to author, Colorado Springs, Colo., May 25, 1973.

12. Hazel Derthick Resmondo to author, Hawthorne, Calif., May 2, 1973, Sept. 24, 1973.

13. Resmondo to author, Sept. 24, 1973; *A History of Beaver County Pioneer Families*, vol. 1 (Beaver, Okla.: Beaver County Historical Society, 1970), pp. 139–40.

14. Jack Names interview.

15. Ibid.

16. Two letters to "Daddy Art," n.d., Names Papers.

17. *History of Beaver County*, 139–40.

18. Resmondo to author, May 2, 1973.

19. Bryon S. Derthick to Art Names, Hawthorne, Calif., n.d., Names Papers.

20. "To Whom it May Concern," n.d., Names Papers.

21. Telegram, Thurston to Art Names, Spur, Tex., Apr. 15, 1944, Names Papers.

22. Tax returns for various years, Names Papers.

23. Worthington interview.

24. Tax returns from various years, Names Papers.

25. Worthington interview.

26. Marian Winter to author, Wichita, Kans., June 11, 1973.

27. Tax returns for various years, Names Papers.

28. Names to Treasury Department, Albert, Okla., Nov. 23, 1937, Names Papers.

29. Rolland Haverstock to author, Wichita Falls, Tex., June 11, 1973.

30. A. F. Lattimore to author, Zenda, Kans., April 11, 1973.

31. Geraldine Bradley Schultz to author, Pampa, Tex., Apr. 24, 1973.

32. "Art Names Comedians," advertising flyer, n.d., Names Papers; *McCracken*

(Kans.) Enterprise, Nov., 1922, as reported in Higgins and Thompson, *McCracken History*, p. 128; Worthington interview.

33. "Art Names Comic Weekly," n.d., Names Papers.

34. H. B. to Art, Wichita, Kans., Feb. 13, 1940, Names Papers.

35. Names to Mr. Reagan, Olton, Tex., Jan. 19, 1940, Names Papers.

36. Bryon S. Derthick to Art, Hawthorne, Calif., n.d., Names Papers.

37. Names to Betty Jo, Olton, Tex., Jan. 25, 1940, Names Papers.

38. Kenneth Whisenhunt interview; Stone interview.

39. Maurine to Dear Pappy, n.d., Names Papers.

40. Derthick to Art, n.d., Names Papers.

41. Art to Maurine, Friona, Tex., n.d., Names Papers.

42. Names to Mr. Reagan, Olton, Tex., Jan. 19, 1940, Names Papers.

43. Art to Betty, Ropesville, Tex., n.d., Names Papers.

44. Art to My Dear Betty, Anton, Tex., Feb. 14, n.y.; Art to Betty, Ropesville, Tex., n.d.; Art to Helen B. & family, Lipscomb, Tex., Mar. 14, 1940, Names Papers.

45. Advertising flyer for *The Fighting Fool!*, n.d.; advertising flyer for *We, Who Are Fools!*, n.d., Names Papers.

46. Worthington interview; Jack Names interview; Jean Names interview; Kenneth Whisenhunt interview.

47. W. H. Fluitt to author, Booker, Tex., Apr. 14, 1973.

48. Art to My Dear Betty, Anton, Tex., Feb. 14, n. y., Names Papers.

49. Art to Helen B. & family, Lipscomb, Tex., Mar. 14, 1940, Names Papers.

50. *Ropes (Ropesville, Tex.) Plainsman*, Apr. 11, 1941.

51. Membership card for 1932, the American Legion, Ben Richardson Post, No. 403, Muleshoe, Tex., Nov. 20, 1931, Names Papers.

52. Art to Mr. Reagan, Olton, Tex., Jan. 19, 1940; Art, Meadow, Tex., to Eastin 16mm Film Co., n.d., Names Papers.

53. *Meadow (Tex.) Star*, undated clipping, Names Papers.

54. King interview; Kenneth Whisenhunt interview.

55. Ibid.

56. Worthington interview; Kenneth Whisenhunt interview; King interview.

57. Worthington interview.

58. Ibid.

59. Jack Names interview.

60. Worthington interview.

CHAPTER 5. ON THE ROAD AGAIN

1. King interview; Kenneth Whisenhunt interview.

2. Worthington interview.

3. King interview; Worthington interview.

4. Kenneth Whisenhunt interview; Lewis Whisenhunt (son of William Whisenhunt), interview by author, Pasadena, Calif., Aug. 5, 1975.

5. Kenneth Whisenhunt interview.

6. Worthington interview.

7. Kenneth Whisenhunt interview; Worthington interview; Jack Names interview.

8. *McCracken (Kans.) Enterprise*, Aug. 27, 1942.

9. Ibid., Sept. 3, 1942.

10. Kenneth Whisenhunt interview; Worthington interview; King interview.

11. Jack Names interview; Kenneth Whisenhunt interview.

12. Jack Names interview; Jean Names interview; Kenneth Whisenhunt interview; Lewis Whisenhunt interview.

13. Tax Return, 1944, Names Papers; Kenneth Whisenhunt interview.

14. Tax Return, 1944, Names Papers.

15. Jack Names interview; Jean Names interview.

16. Kenneth Whisenhunt interview; Lewis Whisenhunt interview; Jack Names interview.

17. Worthington interview; Kenneth Whisenhunt interview.

18. King interview; Kenneth Whisenhunt interview; Jack Names interview.

19. Jack Names interview.

20. King interview; Worthington interview.

21. Worthington interview.

22. King interview; Worthington interview.

23. Kenneth Whisenhunt interview.

24. Worthington interview; Jack Names interview; Kenneth Whisenhunt interview.

25. Worthington interview.

26. Jack Names interview.

27. Kenneth Whisenhunt interview; Lewis Whisenhunt interview.

28. Worthington interview; Jack Names interview; King interview.

29. W. H. Fluitt to author, Booker, Tex., Apr. 14, 1973.

30. Kenneth Whisenhunt interview; Jack Names interview; Mrs. Joe York to author, Garden City, Kans., May 1, 1973.

31. Jack Names interview; Kenneth Whisenhunt interview.

32. Kenneth Whisenhunt interview; Worthington interview.

33. Lewis Whisenhunt interview.

34. Jack Names interview; Jean Names interview; Kenneth Whisenhunt interview.

35. Kenneth Whisenhunt interview; Lewis Whisenhunt interview; Jack Names interview; Jean Names interview.

36. Kenneth Whisenhunt interview.

37. King interview; Lewis Whisenhunt interview; Worthington interview.

38. Kenneth Whisenhunt interview; Lewis Whisenhunt interview; King interview; Worthington interview.

39. Jean Names interview.

40. Art, Jr., to Jack and Jean, Fort Benning, Ga., n.d., Names Papers.

41. King interview.

42. Kenneth Whisenhunt interview; Lewis Whisenhunt interview; Jack Names interview; Jean Names interview.

43. Kenneth Whisenhunt interview; Lewis Whisenhunt interview; Jean Names interview.

44. King interview; Worthington interview.

45. Worthington interview; Kenneth Whisenhunt interview.

46. Jean Names interview; Jack Names interview; Kenneth Whisenhunt interview.

47. Mrs. Joe York to author, Garden City, Kans., May 1, 1973.

48. C. H. Bloomenshine "To Whom This May Concern," Mulvane, Kans., Sept. 15, 1939, Names Papers.

49. Jack Names interview.

50. Ibid.; Jean Names interview.

51. Worthington interview.

52. King interview; Kenneth Whisenhunt interview; William A. Whisenhunt, Jr., letters to his parents.

53. King interview; Kenneth Whisenhunt interview; telegram, War Department to Mr. & Mrs. William Whisenhunt, Apr. 14, 1945.

54. Jack Names interview.

55. Kenneth Whisenhunt interview; Lewis Whisenhunt interview.

56. Jack Names interview.

57. Jack Names interview; Jean Names interview.

58. Kenneth Whisenhunt interview; Jack Names interview.

59. Jack Names interview.

60. Kenneth Whisenhunt interview; Jack Names interview; Jean Names interview.

61. Jack Names interview.

62. Ibid.

63. Ibid.

64. Jean Names interview.

65. Jack Names interview.

66. Jean Names interview.

67. Ibid.; Jack Names interview.

CHAPTER 6. CHARACTER, POLITICS, AND POETRY

1. Worthington interview; Jack Names interview; Jean Names interview; Stone interview.

2. Kenneth Whisenhunt interview; Jack Names interview.

3. H. B. to Art, Wichita, Kans., Feb. 13, 1940, Names Papers.

4. Stone interview.

5. Ibid.

6. Jack Names interview.

7. King interview; Kenneth Whisenhunt interview; Jack Names interview.

8. King interview.

9. Kenneth Whisenhunt interview.

10. Jack Names interview.

11. Odell Hogan to author, Tahoka, Tex., Apr. 27, 1973, May 25, 1973.

12. Stone interview.

13. Kenneth Whisenhunt interview.

14. Ibid.

15. Jean Names interview.

16. Jack Names interview.

17. Stone interview.

18. King interview.

19. Jack Names interview.

20. Jean Names interview.

21. Worthington interview.

22. Several letters between Names and Betty Jo, Names Papers.

23. Various documents in Names Papers; most are untitled and undated and seem to be various revisions of a political statement.

24. For more information on the Nye committee, see Wayne S. Cole, *Senator Gerald P. Nye and American Foreign Relations* (Minneapolis: University of Minnesota Press, 1962).

25. "We Are About to Engage in Another War to Make the World Safe for Democracy," undated document in Names Papers.

26. Untitled and undated document in Names Papers.

27. Ibid.

28. Ibid.

29. Ibid.

30. Ibid.

31. Ibid.

32. Untitled and undated document in Names Papers.

33. Ibid.

34. Sheryl K. Williams, Kansas Collection, University of Kansas, to author, Feb. 26, 1992; Jim Sherow, Professor of History, Kansas State University, to author, e-mail, Apr. 22, 1994.

35. Art to Betty, Ropesville, Tex., n.d., Names Papers.

36. Advertising flyer for *The Fighting Fool!*, n.d.; advertising flyer for *We, Who are Fools!*, n.d., Names Papers.

37. Art to Betty, Ropesville, Tex., n.d.; Art to "My Dear Betty," Anton, Tex., n.d.; Art to Helen B. & family, Lipscomb, Tex., Mar. 14, 1940, Names Papers.

38. Art to "My Dear Betty," Anton, Tex., n.d., Names Papers.

39. Names to Lida Floyd, Lyons, Kans., Feb. 15, 1911, Names Papers.

40. Ibid., Mar. 18, 1911.

41. Names to Lida Floyd, Tacoma, Wash., Jan. 22, 1918, Names Papers.

42. Zippa Hall to author, LaCrosse, Kans., May 1, 1973.

43. Copy in Whisenhunt files.

44. "Times," copy in Whisenhunt files.

45. Untitled poem, copy in Whisenhunt files.

46. Ibid.

47. "The Common Cuss," copy in Whisenhunt files.

48. Untitled poem, copy in Whisenhunt files.

49. "Am I Immortal?" copy in Whisenhunt files.

50. Ibid.

51. Untitled poem, copy in Whisenhunt files.

52. "To Our Sons," copy in Whisenhunt files.

53. "To My Favorite Soldier," copy in Whisenhunt files.

54. Ibid.

55. "Liberty," copy in Whisenhunt files.

CHAPTER 7. PEOPLE'S PLAYWRIGHT

1. Stone interview.

2. Worthington interview.

3. Odell Hogan to author, Tahoka, Tex., Apr. 27, 1973.

4. Ibid.

5. Geraldine Bradley Schultz to author, Pampa, Tex., Apr. 24, 1973.

6. Stone interview.

7. Don B. Wilmeth, *The Language of American Popular Entertainment* (Westport, Conn.: Greenwood Press, 1981), p. 241.

8. Ibid., pp. 25–26.

9. Worthington interview.

10. Ibid.

11. Copies of these scripts are in Whisenhunt files.

12. *Tyranny of Gold*, copy in Whisenhunt files.

13. *Home Brew*, copy in Whisenhunt files.

14. *Are You a Monkey?*, copy in Whisenhunt files.

15. *A Lady in Distress, Two Black Crows, Amos and Andy*, copies in Whisenhunt files.

16. Advertising flyer for *The Call of the Nude*, Names Papers.

17. *The Return of the Devil, The Call of the Nude*, copies in Whisenhunt files.

18. Advertising flyer for *The Call of the Nude*, Names Papers.

19. Jean Names interview.

20. *Marquita [Deep in the Heart of Texas]*, copy in Whisenhunt files.

21. *We, Who Are Fools*, copy in Whisenhunt files.

22. Advertising flyer for *The Challenge*, Names Papers.

23. Advertising flyer for *Here Comes the Dictator!*, Names Papers.

24. Worthington interview; Jean Names interview; Jack Names interview.

25. *Meadow (Tex.) Star*, undated clipping, Names Papers.

26. *Lest We Forget*, copy in Whisenhunt files.

1. Worthington interview; Jack Names interview.
2. King interview; Kenneth Whisenhunt interview; Lewis Whisenhunt interview.
3. King interview.
4. Ibid.
5. Ibid.; Kenneth Whisenhunt interview.
6. Jack Names interview.
7. Kenneth Whisenhunt interview; Names to Dear Son Jack, Leuders, Tex., Mar. 17 [1945], Names Papers.
8. Jack Names interview.
9. Kenneth Whisenhunt interview.
10. Jack Names interview.
11. Kenneth Whisenhunt interview.
12. Jack Names interview.
13. Ibid.
14. Ibid.
15. Worthington interview.
16. Kenneth Whisenhunt interview; King interview.
17. Tax Return, 1944, Schedule of Fire Loss, Names Papers.
18. Ibid.
19. Kenneth Whisenhunt interview.
20. Ibid.; King interview; Lewis Whisenhunt interview.
21. Names to Collector of Internal Revenue, Leuders, Tex., Mar. 12, 1945, Names Papers.
22. Ibid.
23. Names to Gerene Harmon, Lueders, Tex., Feb. 16, 1945, copy in Whisenhunt files.
24. Jack Names interview.
25. Jean Names interview.
26. Ibid.
27. King interview; Kenneth Whisenhunt interview; Lewis Whisenhunt interview.
28. Jack Names interview; Jean Names interview; Worthington interview.
29. King interview.
30. Certificate of Death, Arthur A. Names, Stamford, Tex., Nov. 16, 1945, copy in Whisenhunt files.
31. Jack Names interview.
32. *McCracken (Kans.) Enterprise*, Nov. 22, 1945.
33. Jack Names interview.
34. Jack Names interview; Jean Names interview.
35. King interview; Kenneth Whisenhunt interview; Lewis Whisenhunt interview.
36. King interview; Kenneth Whisenhunt interview.

BIBLIOGRAPHY

MANUSCRIPT AND OTHER PRIMARY SOURCES

Arthur Names Papers. The Arthur Names Papers fill two wardrobe trunks used by the tent show during its operation. Included are scripts, scattered personal correspondence, financial records, and advertising brochures. The papers are held by the Names family. I was given free access to the material and made microfilm copies of most of it.

Whisenhunt Files. These include correspondence with family, friends, and acquaintances of Arthur Names and William Whisenhunt. There is assorted personal information, including death certificates.

SECONDARY SOURCES

Ashby, Clifford, and Suzanne DePauw May. *Trouping through Texas: Harley Sadler and His Tent Show.* Bowling Green, Ohio: Popular Press, 1982.

Bergquist, Laura. "Show Business in the Sticks." *Coronet Magazine* 19 (Jan., 1946): pp. 121–23.

Cole, Wayne S. *Senator Gerald P. Nye and American Foreign Relations.* Minneapolis: University of Minnesota Press, 1962.

Creason, Joe. "Tent Show." *Louisville Courier-Journal Magazine,* July 18, 1948, pp. 5–7.

———. "The Tent Show Carries On." *Louisville Courier-Journal Magazine,* Aug. 20, 1961, pp. 5–7.

Griffith, Sally Foreman. *Home Town News: William Allen White and the Emporia Gazette.* New York: Oxford University Press, 1989.

Harrison, Harry P. *Culture Under Canvas: The Story of Tent Chautauqua.* New York: Hastings House, 1958.

Higgins, Shirley, and Carolyn Thompson, eds. *McCracken History . . . Through Pictures and Newspaper Accounts.* Hays, Kans.: McCracken Centennial Committee, 1987.

A History of Beaver County Pioneer Families. Beaver, Okla.: Beaver County Historical Society, Inc., 1970.

Horner, Charles F. *Strike the Tents: The Story of Chautauqua.* Philadelphia: Dorrance and Company, 1954.

Johnson, Winifred. "Medicine Show." *Southwest Review* 21 (July, 1936): pp. 390–99.

Lostler, Jeffrey. *Prairie Populism: The Fate of Agrarian Radicalism in Kansas, Nebraska, and Iowa, 1880–1892.* Lawrence: University Press of Kansas, 1993.

Martin, Jerry L. *Henry L. Brunk and Brunk's Comedians: Tent Repertoire Empire of the Southwest.* Bowling Green, Ohio: Popular Press, 1984.

May, Earl Chapin. "Our Canvas Broadway." *Country Gentleman,* May, 1931, pp. 16, 17, 95.

Popkin, Zelda F. "The Tent Show Turns to Sex." *Outlook and Independent* 156 (Sept. 24, 1930): pp. 128–30.

Slout, William Lawrence. *Theatre in a Tent: The Development of a Provincial Entertainment.* Bowling Green, Ohio: Popular Press, 1972.

Spillman, Patricia A. *The Kansas Ethos in the Last Three Decades of the Nineteenth Century.* Emporia, Kans.: Emporia State University, 1988.

Stout, Mildred B. *John Hicks, Jr., 1799–1851, and Caroline Fish, 1800–1860: The Ancestors and Descendants.* Pullman, Wash.: privately published, 1983.

Waugh, Frank A. *Outdoor Theatres.* Boston: Richard G. Badger, 1917.

Wilmeth, Don B. *The Language of American Popular Entertainment.* Westport, Conn.: Greenwood Press, 1981.

Names, Arthur A. (*cont.*)
newsletter, 113; and reading law, 37; recites poems before performance, 88–89; recovery from fire, 147; relationship with Maurine, 60, 64–65, 109; religion of, 107–108; reluctance to leave Kansas, 57; remembered fondly, 103; returns to theater after war, 41–42; risks new show, 73; sends poems to Lida Floyd, 115–17; size of company, 44; starts over after fire, 146–47; starts stage show again, 73–74; and taxes, 62–63; themes of plays, 130–31; tries to save tent from fire, 145; as vice president of the Commercial Club, 39; wants to do one-man show, 56; warms up audience, 85; welcomed in communities, 12; would not take abuse, 104; writes plays for specific people, 127–28; writes plays with political content, 136–40; writes short pieces, 129; as a youngster, 34–36

Names, Arthur A., Jr.: absence from show, 94–95; completes high school, 96; in danger in military, 98; enters military, 93; with father, 64; on Names's race for governor, 114; tries show business after war, 152

Names, Art, Jr. *See* Names, Arthur A., Jr.

Names, Jack: on acting role, 94; closes show and joins brother, 149; college, 96; completes high school in military, 96, 149; conflict with townspeople, 88; confusion about parents, 58–59; on death of Junior Whisenhunt, 98; on father and vices, 106; on father's character, 103–104; on father's personality, 105–106; on father's religion, 107; joins military, 149–50; on Junior Whisenhunt, 86; on Names and other women, 109; on Names fining sons, 106; reaction to

father's death, 149; on relation with town girls, 99–100; on schooling, 95–96; on tent fireproofing, 144; on town's attempts to rescue them, 100–101; on town's attitude toward show, 99–101; on town relations, 99; tries to save tent from fire, 145; on Whisenhunt, 70

Names, Jean: and chest pains, 149; completes high school, 96, 149; confusion about parents, 58–59; father attends church with, 107; gets to know father better, 147; goes to college, 96; helped by church people, 100–101; joins military, 149–50; on life in show, 101–102; on Names and other women, 109; opens new show with father, 147; plays women's roles, 94; on schooling, 95–96; as sickly child, 58; on storms, 93; on town relations, 99; wants Jack to join him, 149

Names, Johnnie, 34

Names, Mary Hicks, 34

Names, Maureen: buys first tent with Art, 56; in California, 95; on candy sales, 89; divorce of, 63–64; finding child-care on road, 57–58; has children, 45; on Junior Whisenhunt, 68, 86; known for elegant appearance, 81–82; on life on the road, 96–97; marries Names, 45; meets Names, 44–45; and Mrs. Whisenhunt, 68; on Names and other women, 109; on Names as playwright, 130; on Names reciting poetry, 89; opens show with son Jack, 147; problems after divorce, 65; reaction to medicine show wagon, 56; reaction to Whisenhunt partnership, 70; relationship with Art, 64–65, 109; relationship with Milburn Stone, 46–47; on reputation of theater people, 46; returns to show, 74, 75; sanitary facilities for, 81; on show